Mysterious Stranger

MYSTERIOUS STRANGER

A BOOK OF MAGIC

DAVID BLAINE

Villard Ⓥ New York

LIBRARY OF CONGRESS CATALOGING-IN-PUBLICATION DATA
Blaine, David
Mysterious stranger / David Blaine.
p.   cm.
ISBN 0-375-50573-3
1. Magic tricks. 2. Blaine, David, 1973- I. Title.
GV1547 .B646 2002
793.8–dc21   2002071382

Villard Books website address: www.villard.com

Printed in the United States of America on acid-free paper

24689753

First Edition
Designed by Metze Publication Design

TO MY MOM

Acknowledgments

Without Larry Sloman, aka Ratso, it's highly unlikely that this book would ever have been completed. I was lucky to find someone as incredibly passionate and dedicated as he is to help me turn my thoughts and ideas into actual words. When we began working on this book, he immediately started studying the history of magic and in a few months was much more knowledgeable about the art than most magicians. I first became aware of Ratso when I read his famous book *On the Road with Bob Dylan*. What was intended to be a yearlong collaboration has turned into a true friendship. I'm lucky to have a guy like Ratso in my life.

There's not much to say about Bill Kalush. Without him I wouldn't be here.

Thanks also to:

Austin Metze, Jen May, and Chris Metze, for making the book as beautiful as I could have ever hoped for

Meg McVey, for the photo research

Michael Deas, for his incredible artistic talent

Bruce Tracy, Katie Zug, Janet Wygal, and everyone at Villard Books

David Vigliano, Lon Rosen, Guy Oseary, Jimmy Nederlander Jr., Ari Emmanuel

Tom Bramlett, Bob Brown, Officer Jimmy Eisele, and Adam Gibgot, for sharing their memories for the book, and Colin Gorman for his dedicated work

Paul Harris, David Williamson, Steve Cuiffo, Harvey Cohen, and Michael Weber

Daryl

Pat Smith, Jill Fritzo, Jake Septimus, Ben Steiner, and the Maltese family

Michael James, my brother, and also Sam Sparks

John Marden, Gertrude Bloom

Also thanks—Rick Rubin

And puzzling thanks to the son of John who nearly stepped off a cliff.

Contents

From the moment I picked your book up until I laid it down, I was convulsed with laughter. Someday I intend reading it.

–Groucho Marx to his friend the author S. J. Perelman

Mysterious Stranger

Chapter i
For Those Who Believe

*For those who believe,
no explanation
is necessary.
For those who do not,
none will suffice.*

—Dunninger

For Those Who Believe

n the 1850s in the North African country of Algeria, a group of Muslim miracle men called the Marabouts were stirring up a revolt among the native tribes, encouraging them to sever their ties to France. The Marabouts accomplished this by doing simple pieces of magic that would whip the local tribesmen into a frenzy, convincing them that they possessed supernatural powers. To preserve order in their colony, the French government didn't send troops to Algeria. They sent a retired magician named Robert-Houdin.

Robert-Houdin traveled around Algeria performing miracles. He produced cannonballs from a hat and money from his fingertips. He made a young native disappear. But he faced his most difficult challenge when he visited a small tribe in the desert. A Marabout sheikh who had heard of his previous feats pulled two guns from his robes and challenged him to a duel. Since Robert-Houdin claimed to be invincible, the Marabout would have the right to the first shot. Thinking on his feet, the French magician postponed the duel until eight o'clock the next morning, claiming that he needed six hours of prayer to refresh his powers.

He didn't pray. He spent two hours preparing for this challenge and then fell asleep. The next morning, he met the Marabout and his entourage in the village square. The street was swarming with Algerians who hoped to see the Frenchman killed. The Marabout produced the guns and loaded them with powder. Then he offered Robert-Houdin a choice of bullets. The magician chose two bullets and, under the watchful eye of his adversary, loaded the guns.

The Frenchman walked fifteen paces from the sheikh and turned to face him without displaying the slightest emotion. The Marabout took careful aim, and pulled the trigger. The pistol fired, and Robert-Houdin smiled. He had caught the bullet between his teeth.

Robert-Houdin then lifted his gun and, instead of pointing it at the frightened Marabout, fired the pistol at one of the buildings on

the square. Whitewash flew, and where the bullet had struck, a large patch of blood suddenly appeared and dripped down the masonry.

The Marabout rushed to the wall, dipped his finger in the red substance, and tasted it. It was blood all right. His arms fell to his sides, and his head bowed. The spectators in the square raised their eyes to the heavens and began muttering prayers. Convinced that the French sorcerer had powers far beyond their own, the Algerians lost faith in the Marabouts, and the uprising began to cease.

Over a hundred years later, a Russian magician was performing on-stage as part of a circus. His wife, who was wearing a beautiful fur coat, stood next to him. The magician took out a gun and aimed it at his wife. The gun discharged, and her coat disintegrated into pieces. As each piece hit the ground, it turned into a living mink. Hundreds of frightened minks started running all over the stage.

In 1937 a magician named Rajah Raboid, whose real name was Ray Boyd, was performing in Maine. He chose a random woman from his audience to come to the stage. When she realized that she was to be sawed in half, she refused. Then Raboid found two willing male volunteers and brought them onstage. He told the audience that he was going to perform the classic Sawing a Woman in Half illusion, but this time he would use one of the male volunteers in place of a

The image that sparked my interest in Houdini and, therefore, magic. The eyes.

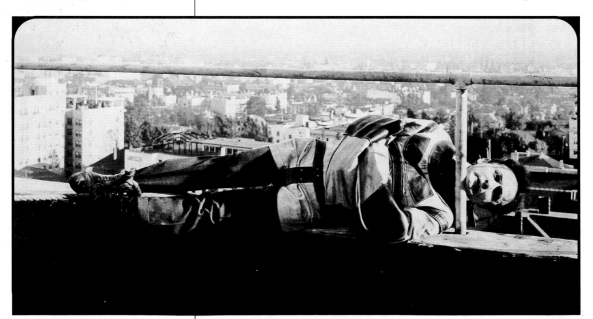

woman. Then he hypnotized one of the men. A box was rolled on-stage. Two assistants helped lift the hypnotized volunteer into the receptacle. The doors of the box were closed, and Raboid began to saw the box containing the man in half.

Suddenly the other volunteer objected. "If you're gonna cut him in half, why do you need a box? It must be a trick box," he scoffed. Indignant, Raboid called for his assistants, and they began dismantling the box. All four sides were removed, so that the man was completely visible as he lay on a thin wooden plank.

Raboid got to work. Slowly and methodically, in full view of the audience, he sawed right through the man's body. What happened next was magic at its best. The lower part of the now-severed man's torso rolled off the plank and scurried offstage. The hapless volunteer looked down and realized that the bottom half of his body was missing. "My legs! My legs!" he screamed. "Where are my legs?" With that, the half-man hopped off the plank, landed on his hands, and slowly waddled toward the audience.

Pandemonium broke out. Screams filled the theater. Women fainted; others bolted for the door. The audience that remained watched in horror as the half-man prowled the stage looking for his legs. He spotted one of Raboid's assistants and grabbed at *his* legs. Horrified, the assistant started running offstage, but the half-man ran right after him. Shortly after they both exited, the volunteer who had been cut in half reappeared, his body once again intact, but he looked disheveled and confused, and he stumbled down from the stage, staggered up the aisle, and exited the theater. The crowd was stunned.

Magic is powerful drama and the world is its stage. When people really witness magic, they never forget it for the rest of their lives. I began my quest for magic when I was in a library at age five. I saw a book called *The Secrets of Houdini*. The cover had a photograph of Houdini bound and tied, lying on his side while balancing on the ledge of a roof. He had such an intense look in his eyes; it looked like he was fighting for his life. This image never left my mind. I intuitively understood that magic is an incredible art that in one mysterious moment can make you question everything. Magic strips away logic, it confronts fears, and brings us to a place of constant wonder and enchantment.

Brooklyn, 1978: The first time I experienced a street performer doing magic with ropes

The most beautiful experience we can have is the mysterious.

—Albert Einstein

CHAPTER II

DISCOVERY OF MAGIC

Discovery of Magic

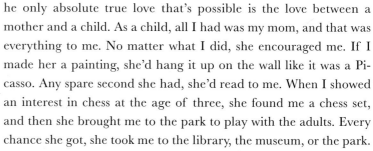

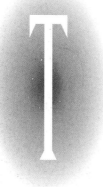

he only absolute true love that's possible is the love between a mother and a child. As a child, all I had was my mom, and that was everything to me. No matter what I did, she encouraged me. If I made her a painting, she'd hang it up on the wall like it was a Picasso. Any spare second she had, she'd read to me. When I showed an interest in chess at the age of three, she found me a chess set, and then she brought me to the park to play with the adults. Every chance she got, she took me to the library, the museum, or the park.

We had a lot of love, but we didn't have it easy. We frequently had to move around Brooklyn because, for some strange reason, the buildings we were living in always burned down. I remember being carried out of a building when I was about three and looking back and watching the whole building go up in flames. In a strange way, this liberated me from material possessions. To this day, these things don't have much meaning to me.

My mother worked three jobs at once just so she could earn enough to send me to a Montessori school. Even though she was juggling all these responsibilities, she still tried to find the time to walk me through the park to bring me to school every morning.

You don't get into magic. Magic gets into you. I've been fascinated by the art for as long as I can remember. Part of my love for magic is about the mystery and science behind it. It also has to do with astonishment and control. It was as if my hands had an independent need to manipulate things. Even right now, I have the urge to go get a deck of cards and play with them. When I was young we didn't even have the means to keep me in magic. My grandmother had given my mother an amazing deck of Tarot cards. They were regulation-size cards with the mysterious Tarot figures depicted on them. The cards were old and yellowed, but that only seemed to add to the mystical feel that they had.

I played with those cards wherever I was, even at the library, where I spent hours upon hours reading every book on magic that I

My mother and me in Brooklyn in 1973

"He was graduated from the finest school, which is that of the love between parent and child. In this school we learn the measure not of power, but of love; not of victory, but of grace; not of triumph, but of forgiveness." —Mark Helprin

Fig. 2.1

could get my hands on. When I was about six, I took the subway to school alone. It was simple; there was one train that I had to take two stops, and the school was right there when I came out of the exit. That morning I was on the train, playing with my cards, when two older ladies took an interest in me. I started doing magic to them, and they were astonished. I was in the middle of a card effect when the subway braked suddenly and the cards fell to the floor. By the time I had collected every one of those precious cards, I'd missed my stop. I tried not to panic, but I was totally lost. Lucky for me, those two ladies took me off the train, walked me across the platform, got on the next train with me, got off, walked me up to my classroom, and explained to the teacher why I was late. I guess even when I was that age my magic had an effect on people.

Not only did I live and breathe magic but I even dreamed about it. From the time I was three years old, I kept having this recurring dream. I was alone in a mysterious place where magic resided. It was like a repository, sort of an enchanted forest, except it was a room that was filled with magic. There were all these huge display cases, made out of glass and the finest mahogany, and they contained the most amazing magical effects. Every type of magic I could conceive was in this sacred place. There were coins that squirted water, and fabulous-looking decks of cards. There was disappearing ink and huge wooden mechanical figures that would do wondrous effects. This wasn't a store; it wasn't like you could just buy these things. It was as if you could somehow obtain magical power just by being there.

I guess I kept dreaming about this magic space because I didn't have the resources to just go into a magic store and buy the latest prop. The ironic thing is that as I got older and began to get more serious about magic, the magic room in my dreams got smaller and smaller. Then after I became a magician, when I finally became a purist and refused to use trick decks of cards or trick objects, when I would do my card effects only with a straight deck, I never had that dream again.

I was only five years old when I told my mom that I was going to be a showman. I had been walking home from school and passed an old man from our neighborhood who spent most of his time sitting on the stoop outside his house. He never really interacted with anybody, he'd just stare vacantly out at the street, so people thought he was pretty odd and they'd just pass him by. For some reason, I walked up to him and asked him if he wanted to see a little magic. I took out my mom's Tarot deck and did a card effect for him. When I finished, he looked at me and started laughing. Before this, I'd never seen him display any emotion. For the first time I felt that incredible electric rush that you experience when your magic really affects someone. I ran home and told my mom that I wanted to do magic for the rest of my life.

She smiled and said that sounded great. It was that kind of unconditional love and respect that gave me confidence that no matter what obstacles came forth, I would be able to succeed in whatever I wanted to do. What I wanted to do was magic.

From an early age I loved playing with reality and making people question their basic beliefs. I used to do that all the time. Most of my mom's friends were deep into things like macrobiotics and metaphysics, so they were naturally open to the unexpected. When I'd take out my Tarot deck and do a card effect, using these mysterious cards just added to the power of the presentation. Sometimes I'd pause in the middle of the effect and just stare, as if I was tapping into some unseen forces. (I'd really be thinking about what I was going to do next.)

I'd set up some amazing coincidences and then blow them off as if they were perfectly normal. I might synchronize my watch with someone else. At a prearranged time, my mother and her friends would be sitting around the kitchen, and suddenly I'd stare at the phone and say, "Phone's about to ring." At that precise moment, the phone started ringing. The women looked at one another in shock. "Is this normal?" they'd ask my mom. She'd play along with it, which really got them wondering.

As soon as I could read I started collecting books that featured optical illusions. This is one of my favorites. Stare at the center of Figure 2.1 for thirty seconds without deviating your gaze. Then look away and stare at a white wall.

Some of my favorite images are the paintings of Salvador Dalí, which to me represent the mind of a great magician. His art had so

Fig. 2.2

Fig. 2.3

many illusions woven into it. I also like the puzzle card image of the face of Vanity—an image that alternated between being a woman at her vanity mirror and being a stark human skull (see Figure 2.2).

One of the first things I learned about magic was that there is a strong correlation between performing magic and playing chess. The further you plan ahead, the more effective your game or magic will be. If you can anticipate other people's moves and also plan out your own moves, you'll be steps ahead of your audience and able to astound them with regularity. A little misdirection always helps too. Misdirection is a skill that magicians use to make their audience look where they want them to, when they want them to. I remember when I was young and playing chess with adults, if I made a really good move, I'd often pretend that I was angry with myself for committing such a "blunder." Because I seemed aggravated, I'd throw my opponents off, they'd overlook my possibilities, and bam, next move I'd take their queen. This is a form of time misdirection, relaxing your opponent's attention and therefore controlling it.

I also found a correlation between magic and science. Many of my earliest magic effects were based on simple scientific principles that would seem miraculous to an audience that wasn't aware of them. I found old yellowed books in the library that were full of these scientific experiments. For example, you can astound people by breaking a glass solely with your voice. It's easy. You strike a cutglass goblet with your finger to make it ring. Then, while it's still vibrating, grab the glass, put it close to your mouth, and shout a

similar sound into it. Since the vibrations are doubled, the glass will invariably shatter.

It's easy to make eggs enter bottles once you're aware of the underlying physics involved. If you heat the contained air in an airtight vessel and immediately seal it, you can create a partial vacuum. The internal air contracts when it cools, and the ensuing partial vacuum can produce great effects. Let's make an egg enter a bottle. First, take a hard-boiled egg and soak it in vinegar so the shell gets softened. Then light a small piece of paper and throw it into an empty wine carafe. Place the egg on top of the carafe to seal it. After a few minutes, the egg starts to elongate and then explodes as it's sucked into the bottle (see Figure 2.3).

There's a great old experiment in inertia that goes back to at least the time of Rabelais, who described it in one of his books. Take a broomstick and insert a thick needle into each end. Then balance the needles on the lips of two glasses that are placed on chairs (see Figure 2.4). Make sure that only the needles, not the broomstick, come into contact with the glass. Take a baseball bat and slam it into the center of the broomstick. Because of the laws of inertia, the broomstick absorbs the entire blow. The broomstick breaks in half, but the glasses surprisingly remain intact.

The simple power of suggestion is a key component of magic. Tell a friend that you're interested in testing his reflexes. Tell him you want to blindfold him so his sense of touch will be even more acute. Explain how even a strong sensation such as the sting of a burned match can take seconds for the brain to process, and you want to know how fast his neurons respond. Say that it might take a few seconds for the pain to be felt, but you want him to tell you the instant he feels the least amount of discomfort from the heat of the match head.

Fig. 2.4

Then take a box of old-fashioned wooden matches and, standing right in front of your subject, strike the match, let it flare up, and make a big show of blowing the flame out. Though your subject is blindfolded, he'll feel your breath when you blow out the match. Then tell him you're touching his skin with the burned match. Within seconds, he'll report that the pain from the heat of the match is becoming unbearable. What's amazing is that you never touch him with the match head—you substitute the edge of an ice cube—but he'll still think you're burning him.

With a little knowledge of science, you can produce a great visual effect with some very simple props. Get a candle and light it. When you blow it out, a stream of smoke will emanate from the wick. Most people don't realize that smoke itself is flammable—when you hold a lit match at the top of that column of smoke, it will ignite and the flame will shoot down the smoke, hit the wick, and reignite the candle.

Sometimes the best magic is opportunistic. When the topic of voodoo comes up in a conversation (either naturally or through the power of your suggestion), begin to ad-lib a brief story explaining how in certain cultures there is a belief that you can manipulate people by doing things to representations of them—the principle behind voodoo dolls.

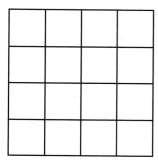

Fig. 2.5

Have a friend make a rough tracing of your right hand on a piece of paper. Make sure that your hand is palm side up and your fingers are spread apart. Tell your friend that the drawing of the hand represents your actual hand. With your right hand out of view, preferably in your pocket, tell her to light a match and hold it over any finger on the drawing of your hand. As she's doing that, suddenly scream "Ouch!" Then smile and tell her that you were just kidding. She'll be amazed, though, when you show her your corresponding finger and the mean-looking blister her match has produced there.

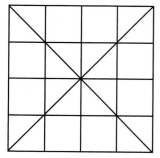

Fig. 2.6

The secret to this effect is that in your pocket you have a key that has a perfectly round key-chain hole. Right after you divert your friend's attention by screaming "Ouch!," you press the key hard into the pad of the finger she's chosen. After a few seconds, the key's hole will cause a "blister" to form on your finger. (If you're performing this for a person who's especially superstitious, you can add little details that will make the effect stronger. Sometimes I'll pull a hair out of my head and place it on the drawing of my hand before

Fig. 2.7

the match is lit. It's a convincing touch for someone who believes in voodoo.)

Now you can demonstrate your own strange powers. Just rub your "blister" as you make an incantation over it. After a few seconds, it's gone—you've healed yourself by the pressure of your rubbing.

Early on I discovered that there were many magic effects based on simple mathematical solutions. One of the most amazing of these is the magic square. Let's say you have a square that consists of four cells to a row, or sixteen cells total. When you add the numbers of any horizontal row, they will be the same. Then, when you add up each vertical row, you'll also arrive at the same number. Even more amazing, the sum of the inner four cells will be the same. The outer four corners will also add up to this sum. Make a three-by-three square and the same thing will be true. Since ancient times magic squares have been reputed to possess mystical powers. In India people would wear magic squares engraved on stone or metal for protection.

Let me show you how to create a magic square. Let's use a four-cell square. Draw a square that contains sixteen cells, four across and four down (see Figure 2.5). Now draw two diagonal lines (see Figure 2.6). Start filling in numbers from left to right, beginning at the top-left cell. But for now, don't put in any numbers that fall on the diagonals. So we don't put in number 1. Put in 2 and 3, but don't put in 4. Put in 5, but omit 6 and 7. Put in 8 and 9. Omit 10 and 11, put in 12. Omit 13. Put in 14 and 15. Omit 16. Your square should look like Figure 2.7.

Now fill in the rest of the cells, starting with 16 (the highest number that was omitted because it was on the diagonal) and working backward. So put 16 in the top-left cell. The next omitted number, 13, goes on the top-right cell. Then 11 and 10 go in the two center cells of the second line from the top; 7 and 6 go below them. Finish filling in the square with 4 and 1. Your magic square should look like Figure 2.8.

Now add up the top four cells. Add the next line. Add the third. Add the fourth. They all add up to 34. Go down now. Go diagonally. They all add up to 34.

It's really a simple formula. You can make magic squares with any number of cells because the magic number of the sum of the cells is arrived at by cubing the number of cells in a row, adding that number to the result, and then dividing the result by 2. In our case,

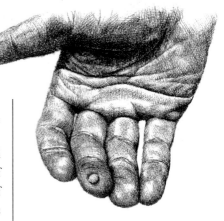

Fig. 2.8

Fig. 2.9

Fig. 2.10

THE STATIC ELECTRICITY DOLLAR BILL EFFECT

Claim that your body is an amazing conductor of static electricity and that you can transfer that power at will. To demonstrate, you'll stand a dollar bill on its edge and knock it down without touching it, simply by moving the charge from your hand to the bill. Here's how it works:

Take a stiff dollar bill, fold it a little in the middle, and put it on a table so that it stands on its own. Take your right hand, rub it on your hair a bit, then rub your hands together vigorously. Now make your right hand stiff like a paddle, with the fingers together. Move it quickly toward the bill, crossing your body from left to right. Stop sharply in front of the bill, with your fingertips pointing directly at the bill as if you're discharging electricity from them. You never touch the bill, but it will fall over.

When spectators try to duplicate the feat, invariably they can't make the dollar move. Of course, your ability to make the dollar fall has nothing to do with static electricity. The dollar will fall because you've made your hand into a paddle and displaced enough air to knock it down. Rubbing your head or your hands together just serves to throw your audience off. The key is the crossing action, which creates the air displacement. Most people will believe it's the static electricity that's knocking the bill down, so they'll be so concerned with rubbing their hands together and making their right hand into a straight paddle that they won't perceive the necessary crossing motion. They'll deliver a straight karate chop toward the bill, displacing very little air, and the dollar will still stand.

4 times 4 times 4 equals 64. Adding 4 gives us 68. Dividing 68 in half gives us our magic number of 34. If you were to make a five-cell square, your magic number would be 65 (5 cubed, plus 5, divided by 2).

Look at your filled-in magic square. Notice that you can transpose individual four-cell units as long as you do it consistently and still have your magic sum of 34. For example, make a new, blank sixteen-cell square. Now make another magic square with different numbers in each cell. Divide the original square into four quadrants. Starting with the 8 in the upper-right quadrant, and going counterclockwise, write those numbers in the first column of your blank square, going from top to bottom. So you'll fill in 8, 13, 3, and 10. Now go to the upper-left quadrant of your original square and fill in the second column of your new square, top to bottom. You'll write in 11, 2, 16, and 5. Now go to the bottom-left quadrant and fill in the third column: 14, 7, 9, and 4. The last column comes from the bottom-right quadrant: 1, 12, 6, and 15. The new magic square also adds up to 34 in any direction.

Now let's combine magic squares with an effect that will leave your audience convinced you're smarter than the top Mensa members. The first thing you'll have to do is memorize the square you just created (see Figure 2.9). I find that the simplest way to do that is to memorize the numbers in groups, going from left to right. So you'd memorize 8, 11, 14, and 1 as one group; 13, 2, 7, and 12 as the second; and so on. Now grab a piece of paper, a pen, and a friend you want to astound. Draw a blank four-by-four square. Look your friend in the eye and say, "I have this amazing power with numbers. I don't even know where it comes from. But you can think of a number between 20 and 75 and I can *instantaneously* create a magic square in which, no matter which way you add up the numbers, they will come to the number you've thought of. Are you thinking of a number?"

When you give the choice of any number between 20 and 75, emphasize the higher number. Odds are he'll pick a higher number. If he chooses any number less than 34, you'll have to tell him to go higher. If he chooses 34, you'll have your magic square already memorized. If it's a number higher than 34, while your friend answers you start filling in the square.

Here's the secret. You simply subtract 21 from the number your

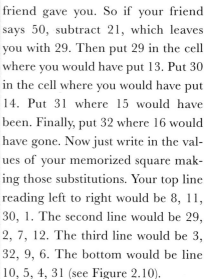

A European magician from the early 1700s producing a bird

friend gave you. So if your friend says 50, subtract 21, which leaves you with 29. Then put 29 in the cell where you would have put 13. Put 30 in the cell where you would have put 14. Put 31 where 15 would have been. Finally, put 32 where 16 would have gone. Now just write in the values of your memorized square making those substitutions. Your top line reading left to right would be 8, 11, 30, 1. The second line would be 29, 2, 7, 12. The third line would be 3, 32, 9, 6. The bottom would be line 10, 5, 4, 31 (see Figure 2.10).

Then do the math for your friend. Every column adds up to his number, 50. The diagonals add up to 50. The two center squares of the top row added to the two center squares of the bottom row total 50. The middle two squares of the first vertical column added to the middle two squares of the last vertical column add up to 50. The pan-diagonals (29, 11, 4, 6) add up to 50, as do the other pan-diagonals (3, 5, 30, 12). Now make four three-by-three squares from your original square. The four corner numbers (8, 30, 3, 9) equal 50, as do the corner numbers of the other three three-by-three squares.

I loved doing math-based magic when I was young, but nothing rivaled my fascination with card effects. Let me show you one of the first effects I learned. Go get a deck of cards. Okay, shuffle it a few times. Good. Deal two piles of cards, one for you and one for me, with no more than about ten cards in each pile. Make sure the piles have equal numbers of cards. Okay. Point to your pile. Pick up the entire pile and look at the bottom card. Got it? There's no way that I could know your card, right? Now put that pile on top of the deck you were just dealing from. Now I want you to take that big deck, and every time I say "Deal," I want you to deal a card and make a brand-new pile on the table, face down. Okay? Every time I say "Deal," you'll put one card, face down, into this new pile.

Ready? Deal. Deal. Deal. Deal. Deal. Deal. Deal. Deal. Deal.

Deal. Deal. *Stop!* Now pick up that entire new pile and put it back on top of the deck you dealt from. Did that? Put my pile on top of the big deck. Now you have the whole deck, right? Okay. You agree there's no way that I could know where your card is, right? Now, I want you to spell out a sentence, dealing down one card at a time from the top of the deck for each letter. For our purposes, let's spell out "This is my card." For each letter, you'll deal another card face down from the top of the deck. Start. T-H-I-S-I-S-M-Y-C-A-R-D. Turn over that last card. That's your card.

A clever way to uncork a bottle of wine. This image is from Gaston Tissandier's late-nine-teenth-century book, Popular Scientific Recreations.

CHAPTER III

THE THREE MAGI

If this is magic,
let it be an art.

—William Shakespeare

The Three Magi

here was a time when magicians were so well respected that kings and queens and even pharaohs would ask them to do command performances. The first recorded magic exhibition took place almost five thousand years ago when Cheops, the pharaoh who presided over the building of the Great Pyramid, summoned a magician named Dedi to his palace. He was said to be able to restore decapitated heads and make wild beasts obey him. It was also rumored that Dedi was 110 years old and that he ate five hundred loaves of bread and a whole shoulder of beef, and drank a hundred jugs of beer, every day.

The pharaoh wanted to see Dedi do his famed decapitation, so he offered the magician a condemned prisoner, but Dedi refused to decapitate a human. Instead he randomly chose a goose from the pharaoh's menagerie. He grabbed the goose's body with one hand and with the other pulled its head off. He then extended his arms, demonstrating that the goose's head was no longer connected to its body. Then he laid the goose's limp body on the floor, walked a few paces away, and set the head down on the ground. After everyone could observe that the decapitated goose was dead, he put the body under one of his arms and walked back over to the head and picked it up. He slowly pushed the lifeless head onto the body and suddenly the goose squawked, full of life, and ran around the room.

The pharaoh was so delighted that he wanted the feat repeated, so Dedi decapitated and restored a pelican. Legend has it that Dedi also hypnotized a lion, after which the docile lion followed the conjurer around like a tame house cat.

Dedi had made his reputation by doing a few amazing feats with animals. I became intrigued by performers who could do one amazing effect they had mastered, as opposed to ordinary magicians who ran through a succession of mediocre illusions. In Houdini's book *Miracle Mongers and Their Methods: A Complete Exposé of Fire Eaters, Heat Resisters, Poison Eaters, Venomous Reptile Defiers, Sword Swal-*

VERA EFFIGIES Dᵐⁱ BLASII DE MANFRE NETINI SICULI Ætia 72.16 51.

Pub'.Nov'.1.1794. by Caulfield & Harding.

Blaise de Manfre achieved fame in the sixteenth century for his miraculous feats of water-spouting. Water spouters hold nearly two gallons of water in their stomachs, then expel the water ten to fifteen feet in high arcs.

lowers, *Human Ostriches, Strong Men, Etc.* (Etc.?), there were a few who left a strong impression on me.

These mind-blowing mystifiers included a voluptuous vaudevillian "rattle-snake poison defier" named Evatima Thardo. She would anger the reptile, offer her bare arms and shoulders, and then there would be awed silence "for the thrill of seeing the serpent flash up and strike possessed a positive fascination for her audiences," Houdini wrote. Thardo would coolly tear the viper from her wound, allow one of the attending physicians to extract a portion of the venom, and then inject it into a rabbit that was on hand. Within seconds the rabbit would die in great agony, but Evatima would be blithely unaffected. Houdini hypothesized that her immunity came from performing after ingesting a large quantity of milk on an otherwise empty stomach, the theory being that venom acts directly on the contents of the stomach and changes it into a deadly poison. Houdini never revealed what the milk did.

Many people have performed with fire over the years, but the most interesting character in the history of fire eating and heat resistance was a Frenchman, Ivan Ivanitz Chabert, who was billed as "the Really Incombustible Phenomenon." Chabert performed the then standard heat-resistance effects of drinking boiling oil and molten lead, but he went one step further by also ingesting phosphorus, arsenic, and oxalic acid. Then, donning a woolen coat, he entered a huge oven heated to 600 degrees, armed with some raw steak. He stayed in the oven for five minutes, all the time singing a popular French song. When he emerged, the steaks were well done, and he invited selected members of his audience to dine with him.

Chabert also achieved notoriety for standing in a flaming tar barrel until it was entirely consumed around him, as well as detonating fireworks attached to his body that burned the shirt off his back. After fifteen years of performing, Chabert settled down in New York in 1833. He opened up a pharmacy (the Fire King's Drug Store), changed his name to J. X. Chabert, M.D., and sold a potion that allegedly cured the white plague. He died penniless in 1859 of tuberculosis. I appreciated Chabert's act because he was really risking his life, as opposed to some famous contemporary magicians who do large-scale fire effects that have no meaning for anyone.

Eating fire was spectacular enough, but there have been people who ate something just as elemental—stones. In his book Houdini traced the first reference to stone eating to a Silesian who in Prague in 1006 consumed thirty-six white stones (weighing over three pounds). But the most famous stone eater of all time was an Italian named Francois Battalia. Legend has it that Battalia was born with two pebbles in one hand and one in the other and refused his mother's milk, finally luxuriating in a meal of the pebbles that he had clutched at birth. He then survived for the rest of his life eating only stones, washed down with various liquids. Battalia would put three or four stones in a spoon, swallow them, and chase them with a glass of beer. He would eat about "half a peck" of stones every day, merrily shaking his belly to allow those around him to hear the stones rattling. Once every three weeks he would eliminate a vast quantity of sand.

Chabert the Fire King

In 1788, over a hundred years after Battalia, a performer known as the Original Stone-Eater appeared in England. He refined the art of stone eating by encouraging the audience to bring their own "black flints or pebbles," which the Stone-Eater happily devoured. Battalia and the Stone-Eater were the apotheosis of this arcane art. By Houdini's time, stone eaters were employing shortcuts and devious tricks. After bribing one of these performers, Houdini learned that their secret was a simple one: between shows, the stone eater would take a dose of a powerful laxative and clear his system in time for the next performance. In 1895 a Japanese performer with the San Kitchy Akimoto troupe taught Houdini a method that enabled one to swallow large objects and bring them up later at will. They would practice with very small potatoes and graduate to objects as "large as the throat will receive."

All these bizarre performers fascinated me. Then I read about the dime museums and P. T. Barnum's wonderful complement of midget performers. While Tom Thumb and his midget colleagues were incredible, I soon discovered one of the most amazing showmen who ever graced a stage. His name was Matthew Buchinger, and he was born on either June 2 or June 3, 1674, in Ger-

XAVIER CHABERT.
The Fire King.

Eng.d by W. Holl, from a Drawing by A. Wivell.
London, Published by the Proprietor at the Argyll Rooms Dec.r 26.th 1829.

many, the last of nine children. He grew to only twenty-nine inches in height, but his parents resisted exhibiting him as a freak and he was allowed to lead a more or less normal life. As soon as they died, he began performing.

The Wonderful Little Man of Nuremberg, as he was later known, was a celebrated magician, startling audiences with his tremendous talent for making cork balls disappear from under cups. He played many musical instruments, including some of his own invention, expertly. No one could beat him at cards, and audiences would marvel at his wonderful displays of marksmanship. His versatility even extended to bowling, and he would demonstrate trick shots that seemed impossible. Buchinger was a particular favorite of royalty, performing for the nobility both in England and on the Continent.

Despite his diminutive size, he married four normal-sized women and fathered at least fourteen children. To support this vast brood, he routinely sold his artwork— intricate drawings of landscapes, coats of arms, and portraits. What made this artwork truly special was that embedded in the portraits were amazingly detailed examples of minute writing. A close examination of the curls of hair in a self-portrait would reveal that the shading in the curls of the wig was really complete biblical psalms and the Lord's Prayer, inscribed in miniature letters.

What's even more amazing is that Buchinger was able to perform these diverse feats despite the fact that he had no arms, no legs, no thighs, and no hands. He was basically just a stump of a man, with two small, finlike appendages growing out of his shoulder blades. He certainly made the most of them.

Stone eaters, freaks, fire resisters—the parameters of my magical world were rapidly expanding, but when it came to classic magic, besides Houdini and Orson Welles (more on them later), three men brought the art of magic to a new level. They were Robert-Houdin, Max Malini, and Alexander Herrmann.

LONDON. April the 29.1724. This is the Effigies of Mr. Matthew Buchinger, being Drawn and Written by Himself He is the wonderful Little Man of but 29. Inches high, born without Hands, Feet, or Thighs, June the 2.1674. in Germany, in the Marquisate of Brandenburgh, near to Nurenburgh. He being the last of nine Children, by one Father and Mother, Viz. Eight Sons, and one Daughter. The same little Man has been married four times, and has had Issue eleven Children, Viz. one by his first Wife, three by his second, six by his third, and one by his present Wife.

This little Man performs such Wonders as have never been done by any; but Himself. He plays on various Sorts of Music to Admiration, as the Hautboy, Strange Flute in Consort with the Bagpipe, Dulcimer and Trumpet; and designs to make Machines to play on almost all Sorts of Music. He is no less eminent for Writing, Drawing of Coats of Arms, and Pictures to the Life, with a Pen; He also plays at Cards and Dice, performs Tricks with Cups and Balls, Corn and live Birds; and plays at Shittles or Nine-Pins to a great Nicety, with several other Performances, to the general Satisfaction of all Spectators.

How to be a georgia wonder

In the 1800s two women performers, Lulu Hurst (the Georgia Wonder) and Annie Abbott (the Georgia Magnet), performed feats of strength and resistance using then little-known laws of inertia. Using a similar principle, you can successfully resist the combined strength of ten people. Stand facing a wall, with your arms fully extended and your palms flat against the wall. Make sure your fingers point upward.

Then get ten volunteers and put them in size order, with the smallest one first in line. Have them stand in a single file behind you (remember to make sure the smallest is first), with each one's hands outstretched and placed on the back or shoulders of the person immediately in front of them. On the count of three, have them push with all their might and try to pin you against the wall. Of course they can't, and often their exertions will cause them to be thrown to the ground.

Because of the laws of inertia, each person in line will absorb the pressure of the person directly behind him. The combined force of all the people behind cannot be transferred to the people in front of them, so as long as you can withstand the force of the person who's immediately behind you (the smallest person in the group), you'll be able to hold off the entire team. Just be sure to resist the pressure entirely with your wrists. If you use only your hands, you increase the likelihood of injuring your wrists.

Jean-Eugène Robert (he added Houdin after he married his first wife) was born in Blois, France, on December 7, 1805. His father was a watchmaker, and Robert-Houdin was set to become a lawyer when a strange twist of fate intervened and set him on a magical path. As a youth he had gone into a bookshop to buy a book on clock making. When he got home, he discovered that the bookseller had actually given him a similar-looking book called *Scientific Amusements*, which contained two entire volumes of magic. Reading about conjuring gave Robert-Houdin "the greatest joy . . . ever experienced." He couldn't put the books down. In fact, he stole the town's oil lamp to continue reading well past his bedtime.

For over twenty years Robert-Houdin studied magic, supporting himself as a clockmaker and a creator of automatons. He finally opened his own theater in Paris in 1845 and began a short seven-year magical career that redefined the state of the art. Robert-Houdin's contributions to magic were enormous. He was among the first magicians to replace the ridiculously large cumbersome boxes and stage paraphernalia with a simple, elegant, more natural stage set. He also dressed in evening wear instead of the ludicrous Merlin-inspired pointed hats and robes that some conjurers favored.

Robert-Houdin's theories of magic were what intrigued me the most. His notion that a magician is an actor who plays the part of someone with supernatural powers was revelatory, and his theories on acting seemed to anticipate the Method school. "Although all one says during the course of a performance is . . . a tissue of false-hoods, the performer must sufficiently enter into the part he plays, to himself believe in the reality of his fictitious statements," he wrote. "This belief on his own part will infallibly carry a like conviction to the minds of the spectators."

The great French magician from whom Houdini took his name

These ideas, along with his immaculate attention to detail, made Robert-Houdin's magical effects among the most memorable ever performed. In addition to his many magical innovations, it was the creativity he brought to standard effects that propelled them to a new level of achievement. Take his famous Ethereal Suspension. This was a variation on an old suspension that had been done by Indian fakirs. As if by a miracle, the magician would suspend his assistant in midair, supported only by one pole under one arm. Robert-Houdin took this one step further. Ether had recently been introduced as an anesthetic, so Robert-Houdin claimed that he had discovered a new wonderful property of ether—that it would, in strong enough concentrations, render the body of a human as light as a feather. To demonstrate this, he brought his young son center stage.

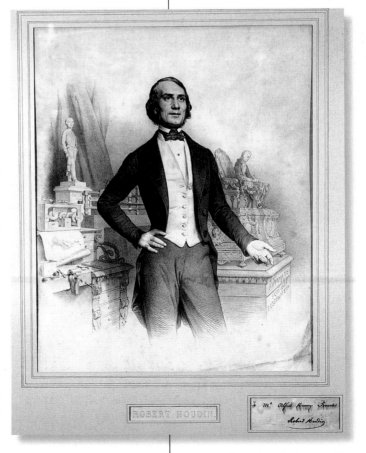

Three stools were placed on a wooden plank that rested on two end trestles. His son stood on the center stool and extended his arms, and canes that rested on the outer stools were placed in his armpits.

Now Robert-Houdin's artistry came into play. A flask that purportedly contained ether was held beneath his son's nose until the boy apparently fell asleep. Thanks to a backstage assistant, who was pouring actual ether onto hot shovels, the smell of the chemical permeated the theater. The center stool was removed, then one of the canes and its supporting stool were removed and, as if by miracle, Robert-Houdin's son was suspended by a single cane. Then, to prove his son's incredible lightness, the magician lifted him to a horizontal position using only his little finger. His son was now sleeping peacefully, lying horizontally, with only a single cane supporting his entire body.

Robert-Houdin's other effects were just as sensational, but his greatest performance took place far from the stage of his small theater in Paris. In the first chapter, I described Robert-Houdin's mission to Algeria on behalf of his government. While his duel with the provincial Marabout leader was amazing, his earlier performance in a small theater in Algiers warrants scrutiny for both the elegance and the power of his effects.

On October 28, 1856, Robert-Houdin found himself facing an audience of Arab chieftains, brigades of native soldiers under French command, translators, and other civilian authorities. His job was to convince them of his supernatural power. He was an actor playing the part of a wonder-worker.

He began by doing nothing. The profound, almost religious silence seemed to petrify the spectators. He then started playing to the Arabs, the part of the audience he had to convert. First he produced cannonballs from a hat—perhaps a sly metaphor for France's military superiority. Then flowers, then five-franc coins, all mysteriously emanating from the simple hat.

At this point, Robert-Houdin would normally perform his famous Inexhaustible Bottle effect, in which a single bottle would produce enough wine to satisfy the entire audience. This evening, he adapted to the customs of the Muslims, who shunned alcohol, and conjured up steaming coffee, which appeared miraculously from a large silver punch bowl. But mere amusement wasn't enough. He had saved for last three effects that would "startle and even terrify" his audience.

Robert-Houdin brought a small box to center stage. "From what you have witnessed, you will attribute a supernatural power to me, and you are right. I will give you a new proof of my marvelous authority by showing that I can deprive the most powerful man of his strength and restore it at my will." He then asked for a volunteer, and a muscular Arab came onstage.

"Are you strong?" he asked the Arab.

"Oh, yes."

"Are you sure that you will always remain so?"

"Quite sure."

"You are mistaken, for in an instant I will rob you of your strength, and you shall become as a little child."

The magician then asked the Arab to lift the box. The Arab did it with ease. "Is that all?" he said coldly.

"Wait," Robert-Houdin said, then made an imposing magical gesture at the Arab. "Behold, you are now weaker than a woman. Now try and lift the box." Unbeknownst to the Arab, the magician had activated a strong electromagnet under the stage. The box had an iron plate in its base, so the magnetic force made it immovable. The Arab strained to lift the box by its brass handle, to no avail. Then the magician delivered the final blow. Robert-Houdin triggered another switch, and a live electric current surged through the handle of the box. The Arab's body went into convulsions, his legs collapsed, and he screamed in agony. The magician mercifully disengaged the current, and the Arab, thoroughly embarrassed, ran out of the theater.

Robert-Houdin then did two more standard effects. He caught a bullet that was fired at him with an apple, and he made a young Moor volunteer disappear from under a large cloth cone. This last

The master magician in his later years

effect so unnerved the audience that there was a general panic and people rushed for the doors, only to be met there by the same young Moor, resurrected by the master wonder-worker Robert-Houdin. The spectacle was so impressive that a few days later the Arab chiefs met with the magician at the governor's palace. They wore red robes, a sign that they would now pledge loyalty to France, and presented Robert-Houdin with a scroll to honor his feats.

The conjurer returned triumphantly to his native land, where he wrote four remarkable books, including his memoirs, which ranks as one of the most influential books on magic. He died of pneumonia in 1871, but his contributions to the art of magic reverberate to this day.

Max Malini was the polar opposite of Robert-Houdin, but in some respects he was his equal as a magician. Whereas Robert-Houdin was cultured and debonair, Malini was crude and blunt, but his small, stubby hands produced some of the most incredible pieces of magic ever seen. Malini was born Max Katz in Ostrov, on the Polish-Austrian border, in 1873. A few years later his family emigrated to New York City. At age twelve Max became an acrobat, but three years later he learned magic from Professor Seiden, an old fire eater and ventriloquist who owned a bar on the Bowery. In a few short years Malini was performing for royalty, palling around with Enrico Caruso and Al Capone, getting drunk with General John Pershing, and receiving fan mail from President Warren G. Harding.

He accomplished all this despite the fact that he almost never appeared in a theater. Malini was the master of close-up magic, and many of his legendary effects were produced when he was surrounded by a group of people at a bar. Malini would come to a city and do impromptu magic at local taverns. When he'd built up a reputation, he would rent a room in a hotel, sell multiple tickets to the newfound friends he had mystified, and then do a two-hour show for the hundred or so people who would show up. His props were simple—cards, coins, lemons, and handkerchiefs—but in his hands the results were miraculous.

Almost all of his success could be chalked up to rigorous preparation. What seemed spontaneous to his amazed spectators was well planned in advance. Malini would stand at a bar and regale his audience with stories of his worldwide travels. During the conversation, the magician might innocently inquire his companion's age.

When the man told him, Malini would scoff. "Vat! I don't beleef you. Let me see your hair." The man would proudly lift off his hat to reveal his full head of hair, and while he did so, Malini would surreptitiously load a playing card into the man's hat. Later, he would pull out a deck of cards, force the same man to pick a duplicate of the card, vanish it, then dramatically find it in the man's hat.

Malini was handicapped by his small hands, which weren't even large enough to palm standard-sized playing cards, but he more than made up for this difficulty by his amazing skills at misdirection. When asked by a friend how he could fool so many people with his sleights, Malini replied, "Vell, you don't do it ven they're vatching."

"What do you mean?" his friend probed.

"I vait. I vait."

"How long do you wait?" the friend asked.

"I'll vait a veek." Malini shrugged.

Sometimes he waited even longer to pay off an effect. One day he was in a fashionable tailor shop in Washington, D.C., when he noticed a formal suit with a tag on it. Malini recognized the owner as a prominent U.S. senator. He immediately befriended the owner of the shop and before long persuaded the owner to sew a playing card into the lining of the suit. Who knows how long Malini waited until he was in the presence of the same senator so he could amaze him by producing that card from the inside of his jacket?

The most famous story involving Malini took place at an elegant dinner party at the home of an English duke. Before the dinner the magician had somehow managed to sneak into the kitchen carrying a live chicken whose feathers had been removed. It's easy to believe that Malini beguiled the kitchen staff with some great magic and got them to go along with his stunt. He pretended to hypnotize the bird (he probably slipped it some tranquilizers) and applied a paste so that it would look roasted to a golden brown. Then he placed it on a platter, surrounded it with potatoes and vegetables, and instructed the kitchen staff to bring out this loaded bird at mealtime. They did.

At the table, Malini had steered the conversation to speculations about resurrection and reincarnation. The bird arrived and, thanks

A young, hustling Malini. He gained prominence when he jumped on a train to Washington, D.C., spotted an influential U.S. senator on the street, approached him, and bit a button off his suit. The senator was upset and outraged, but Malini said, "Vait," and proceeded to spit the button back onto the jacket, restoring it to its original position. The senator was so amazed that he watched while Malini did more incredible close-up magic, then invited him to do his magic for Congress. Soon Malini was performing in the White House.

to the subdued lighting, nothing seemed out of the ordinary. Then, just as the servant was about to carve the chicken, Malini interrupted. "Meester Duke, I show you a leetle trick." He made a few mysterious passes at the bird and then nodded to commence carving. As the knife entered the fowl, the bird woke up, squawked furiously, and scrambled off the table. The guests all ran screaming out of the room.

Malini made and spent many fortunes in his life. Eventually he moved to Hawaii, where he spent his last days entertaining American servicemen, so weak that he had to sit on a chair while he performed. He died on October 3, 1942, of malnutrition. His motto was "You'll wonder when I'm coming. You'll wonder more when I'm gone."

That same wonder always surrounded Alexander Herrmann. To many scholars of magic history, Herrmann was the complete magician. He was tall and thin, and his grandiose mustache, pointy beard, and piercing eyes gave him a Mephistophelian appearance that helped create the classic stereotype of a magician. Herrmann always said that magicians were born and not made, and it was certainly true in his case. His father, a German-born physician, dabbled in magic, entertaining both the sultan of Turkey and Napoleon. Alexander was born in Paris in February 1843 and began his magic career at the age of ten, when he left his family and joined his eldest brother, Carl (Compars), who was then performing in Russia. He was levitated in one effect and demonstrated "second sight" mind-reading ability in another.

A few years later Alexander began his own show. He toured Europe, performing, like his brother before him, for both the general public and royalty. A linguist, Alexander spoke French, English, German, Spanish, Italian, Dutch, Russian, Portuguese, Chinese, Arabic, and Swedish—giving him access to a much wider audience than most magicians had. He was also proficient in the arcane art of card throwing, powerful enough to bounce cards off the rear walls of large theaters, yet accurate enough to scale a card into the lap of any given audience member.

What made Herrmann such a compelling figure in the history of magic was that he took Robert-Houdin's dictum to heart; he was the consummate actor playing the part of a miracle worker. Herrmann never broke character—magic surrounded him wherever he was. He'd visit a street vendor and amaze her by breaking open a few of her eggs and plucking gold coins from them. He'd lift his glass to toast friends at dinner, and suddenly it would vanish into thin air, only to resurface in someone's coat. When the mayor presided at his wedding ceremony in City Hall in New York, Herrmann paid for the license by pulling a wad of cash from Hizzoner's sleeve. On being introduced to President Ulysses S. Grant, he reached up and pulled a handful of cigars from the president's beard. When the czar of Russia demonstrated his skill by tearing a deck of cards in half, Herrmann merely shrugged, piled one half on top of the other, and tore the deck into quarters.

Alexander Herrmann

He'd also use his magic to defuse potentially embarrassing situations. One day when Herrmann was working at a theater owned by the impresario Oscar Hammerstein, one of his assistants accused the famous promoter of coming backstage to steal Herrmann's secrets. Hammerstein was indignant and, to mollify him, Herrmann took a diamond-studded locket, wrapped it in a piece of paper, and offered it to Hammerstein as a gift. "Keep this and remember me by it." He smiled at the owner. Later, in the privacy of his office, Hammerstein opened the package. Instead of the locket, he found an old railway ticket.

Herrmann was fully aware of the publicity value that his street magic afforded, so the day before his show he would often put on a display of his powers for local reporters. He also had an irrepressible sense of humor that was manifested in some now legendary stunts. One night when he was in New York he was part of a crowd watching an Indian fakir perform stunts in Union Square. Seeing two kids enthralled by the spectacle, Herrmann waited until a strolling police officer neared them. Then he pickpocketed a watch from one of the young men, leaving the chain dangling from his vest. Herrmann then gave the chain a yank and waited for the inevitable results.

The young man, seeing his watch was gone, screamed out. Herrmann, looking guilty, started to edge away. The youth grabbed him and, of course, the police officer rushed over, and they all wound up

Hadji Ali would drink nearly two gallons of water, then swallow a glass of kerosene, which would float on top of the water in his stomach. First he'd spout out the kerosene at a small fire, feeding the flames. Then he'd regurgitate the water, putting out the fire. This clip is from his performance in the 1931 Laurel and Hardy movie Politiquerias.

at the nearest precinct, where a sergeant tried to sort things out. "This guy stole my watch," the kid vowed. Herrmann denied it. In fact, he stated, it was the youth who was the perpetrator. "Where is your badge, officer?" Herrmann asked the beat cop. The cop was shocked to find that his badge was missing. "This man who accuses me stole your badge. I saw him take it. Search him, you'll see," the magician said. "You're a liar," the "victim" screamed but then fell silent when, after rummaging through his pockets, he found the badge.

"Now, officer, see what else is gone. A man who'd steal a badge would steal anything," Herrmann predicted. It didn't take long for the officer to turn white when he realized his gun was missing, and for the gun to show up in the pocket of the friend of the "victim." Herrmann wasn't through yet. "And now for this watch business. I think you'd better search yourself," he said to the arresting officer. Needless to say, the watch was in the cop's jacket pocket. "You see"—Herrmann smiled, turning to the desk sergeant—"I'm the only honest man among them all."

At a dinner at a private club in Chicago, Herrmann made wine bottles disappear into thin air, found a missing playing card in the shoe of an archbishop, and chided the club president for stealing his shoes. "My feet are getting cold," he protested, then reached out his hand and pulled his shoes from inside the shirt of the hapless president. Herrmann was the supreme master of impromptu magic, but even he was bested once. One night he was introduced to Bill Nye, a celebrated humorist. At dinner Herrmann leaned over and, foraging through Nye's salad, uncovered a large diamond. "Dear me, how careless," the magician deadpanned, but Nye was too quick. He grabbed the diamond. "I'm always leaving things like that around.

Waitress, here's a little present for you." Nye handed her the gem. It took a lot of explanation before Herrmann was able to get the restaurant manager to convince the waitress to return the stone.

Herrmann mystified audiences for over forty years. He set a record in London, performing for a thousand nights consecutively. He crisscrossed the Continent many times. In fact, in 1885, at a sit-down in Paris, Alexander and his brother Carl divided up the magic world. Carl would perform exclusively in Europe, while his younger brother would have the exclusive rights to the Americas. Alexander settled down with his wife and an assistant in a mansion in Long Island, along with a bevy of cats, dogs, ducks, pigeons, geese, and blue monkeys, but no children. To compensate, he made many visits to orphanages, where he delighted the kids with wonderful magic.

He was also incredibly generous, with both his time and his money, toward all charitable endeavors. On December 16, 1896, Herrmann was set to perform in Rochester, New York, when he heard that a theater group whose production was a bust was stranded in that city. Without solicitation, Herrmann paid the entire troupe's hotel bills and railroad fares back to their homes. Then he visited a local juvenile prison and put on an impromptu show before his presentation that evening. He died the next day of a heart attack, on his private railroad car, en route to another performance. His body was returned to New York, and at his funeral thousands of people jammed the streets to get a glimpse of his coffin. The following day the *New York World* decreed that "magic itself" had died with Herrmann.

CHAPTER IV

SECRETS
OF CARDS

Oh what a tangled web we weave,
When first we practice to deceive!

—Sir Walter Scott

Secrets of Cards

Winston Churchill had the weight of the world on his shoulders. World War II was entering its darkest hour, and the English prime minister was in the middle of a complex strategy session on how to deal with the Nazi threat when a few of his friends intervened and took him to dinner. Even through the meal Churchill was preoccupied with his life and death decisions, so as soon as the dessert was finished, he started to rush back to a meeting with Parliament members, but his friends insisted that he stay for a few minutes more. There was some entertainment scheduled.

Churchill reluctantly sat down as the American vaudeville comic Harry Green walked into the room. He approached the prime minister, but instead of breaking into a skit he broke out a deck of cards. Green was also a conjurer, and this was his chance to beguile Churchill with an effect called Out of This World, something many experts acknowledge as the greatest card effect ever produced.

Green opened a new pack of cards, discarded the jokers and took one red card and one black card out of the deck. He put them six inches apart, face up on the table in front of Churchill. Handing the rest of the deck to the prime minister, he instructed him to deal out the cards, one at a time. If Churchill believed the card was a red card, he should put it face down on top of the red card on the table. If he instinctively felt that it was a black card, he should put that one face down on top of the black card. He was to repeat this process for the rest of the deck.

Churchill complied. Soon there were two piles, each resting on the two face-up leader cards. Green then told Churchill that the odds against him correctly sorting out the deck into a black and a red pile were more than 200 trillion to one. You can imagine Churchill's surprise when the cards were turned over and the deck had been perfectly separated into black and red cards.

Suddenly the war was put on hold. Churchill repeated the

(opposite page) *Caravaggio's* The Cardsharps, *the first great painting on the subject of cheating*

whole effect, concentrating on each card as he guessed its color. To his amazement, he had once again perfectly divided the cards. He repeated the effect over and over and over, and each time the same miracle transpired. It wasn't until 2:00 A.M. that a completely befuddled Churchill finally arrived for his meeting at the Houses of Parliament, looking, in the words of the London *Times* reporter, "befogged."

Go get a deck of cards. By the end of this chapter, I'll teach you a few card effects that I am sure will leave your audience just as bewildered as Churchill was. Take the cards out. Run them through your hands. To most magicians, cards themselves are marvels. The great card magician Dai Vernon said that a pack of cards should be treated like a living, breathing thing. For one thing, they feel special in your hand. Touching them, holding them, shuffling—the whole process is almost poetic. If you're in a room full of magicians and someone just mentions the word *cards,* within seconds, everyone is digging into their pockets and pulling out a deck of cards. It's one of the most amazing feelings ever. People as diverse as Woody Allen, Orson Welles, Johnny Carson, and former Bear Stearns chairman Ace Greenberg all are or have been into doing card magic.

Cards are nearly ubiquitous tools of amusement. There aren't many people on the planet who don't recognize them. But, as strange as it might seem, playing cards haven't been around since antiquity—in fact, they're a fairly new phenomenon. We don't know for certain when they were introduced, but we know that they didn't come to Europe much before the last quarter of the fourteenth century. At first, they were used for a variety of games—it wasn't until much later that cards were employed to foretell the future.

It comes as no surprise that cards were used as a means of divination when we examine the cards themselves. Whoever designed the first deck of cards seems to have imbued the cards with a not so coincidental astrological significance. For example, the pack is evenly divided into red and black cards—analogous to day and night. The modern pack has fifty-two cards, coinciding with fifty-two weeks in the year. The year has four seasons, the pack four suits. There are thirteen cards per suit, and thirteen lunar cycles per year. Finally, when you add all the points per card (with a jack counting 11, queen 12, and king 13) and giving the joker the value of 1, your total is 365, the number of days in a year.

Almost any card effect seems miraculous when you realize that

US, EG ROT

Fig. 4.1

the number of distinct orders a single pack of playing cards can occupy is absolutely staggering. Since you have fifty-two cards in a deck, that number would be 52 factorial, which is equivalent to 8.1 times 10^{67}. If you add in the factor of having a card face up or face down, the number of permutations of one deck will be about equal to the estimated number of atoms in the universe.

Let's start off with an effect that relies on much more simple mathematics. It's called the Twenty-one Card Effect. I want you to begin by shuffling that deck of cards. Okay, now make three piles of seven cards each. Square the three piles. Cut to a card in any one of the piles, look at it, and remember it. Now drop the pile of cards you have in your hand on either of the other two piles. Cut some cards from the remaining pile and put them on top of the pile with your card. Put the remaining piles on top of that pile so you're left with one pile. Now I want you to deal three cards face up in a row from this pile. After the first row, deal a second on top of it with the cards overlapping downward a little bit. Keep dealing out rows of three cards in this manner until you've dealt all the cards from the pile, creating seven rows. You should be looking at three columns of face-up cards (see Figure 4.1).

Okay, let me think about this. I don't think your card is in column one, so remove all those cards. I know it's not one of the top two cards in column 2, so remove those. There's no way it's any of the bottom four cards in column 3, so remove those. It's not the bot-

tom card of the second column. Get rid of it. It's not one of the top three cards of the third column. We're left with four cards. It's not the top two cards. I don't think it's the bottom card. If I'm right, the one card that's facing you now is the card you cut to in the beginning.

Of course that *has* to be your card. Once you cut to a card and drop that pile on one of the remaining piles of seven cards, your card will be the eighth card from the bottom of the twenty-one-card pile no matter how many times you cut the remaining cards and add them to the master pile. Then, when you deal out the cards face up in three columns, your card will always be in the center column, the third card from the bottom. You've just done my version of a card effect that's over four hundred years old.

Some great card effects are based on simply knowing the bottom card of the deck. This is called the key card principle. Let me give you an example. Sometimes when people shuffle cards, they shuffle them in a way that allows you to see the bottom card. Let's say it's the three of spades. Immediately tell them to hold the deck face down in their hand. Now have them slide one card out of the deck, remember it, and then put it back on top of the deck. Have them cut the deck. They can even cut it again if they want. Now you take the deck and look through the cards. You're looking for the three of spades, and when you find it, you know that their card is the card immediately beneath it (the card whose back touches the face of the three of spades).

Here's another effect that's based on two cards' proximity to each other. You have to do this one with a new or at least a decent deck. It can't be all beat up and humid; the cards should be somewhat slippery. Give the cards to the person you're doing this to and have her shuffle them thoroughly. Then tell her to hold the deck face down in the palm of her left hand. Have her pick up any number of cards from the deck and look at the card she

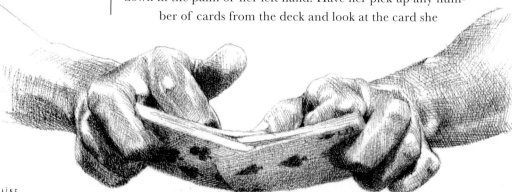

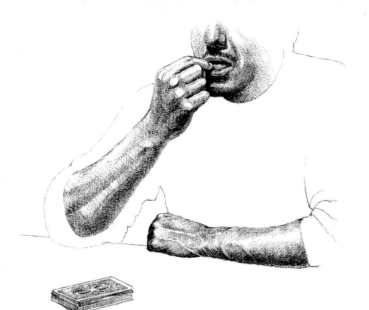

cut to—that's her card. While she's doing this, secretly wet your finger with some spit. You don't want saliva dripping off your finger, but make sure there's ample moisture on it. Since she still has the pile of cards she cut off the deck in her right hand, you touch the top card of the bottom half of the deck (the cards that remained in her left hand) with your wet finger and say, "Now put the top half back here." Tell her to square the deck; she can even cut it. Now she'll feel that her card is legitimately lost in the deck.

Take the deck back. As you hold the cards facing you in the palm of your left hand, push the cards over one at a time with your left thumb. Be gentle. As you spread out the deck, at one point you'll see two cards that are stuck together. Your friend's card will be the left card of those two. What happened was your spit acted as an adhesive and bound those two cards together. The card to the right had your spit on its back, so the card that's clinging to it was the one placed directly on top of the card you loaded with your saliva. Since you made sure to tell your friend to remember her card, her attention is focused on the card she cut to, so she won't see you wet your finger. It's also not unusual for you to gently tap the card where you want your friend to return the cards she cut, so she'll never figure out how you managed to pull off this effect.

The ability to predict what card your audience will choose is an

*Jacques Callot's engraving
depicting card cheats, from
about 1620*

amazing feat. Here's one simple way you can do it. Give someone the cards. Have him shuffle the deck thoroughly. Now take the deck and hold the cards in front of you so no one else can see them. Spread the cards between your hands so you can see most of them. You need to see the top two cards. If they're the same suit or the same value, close the deck, give it a cut, and spread it again.

Look at the top two cards. Let's say the jack of hearts is on top and the ten of clubs is next. Using the value of the top card and the suit of the second card, your prediction will be the jack of clubs. Take that card out of the deck and, without your spectator seeing it, put it face down on the table in front of him. (For added relish, you might put a glass ashtray over it or put it inside the empty box the cards came in.)

Now square the deck up and hand it face down to your spectator. Tell him to deal the cards one at a time face down into one pile. He can deal as many as he wants as long as it's more than two. When he's done, tell him to eliminate the rest of the deck. Now have him take the pile of cards he's just dealt down and deal them into two piles—one for him and one for you. When that's done, have him turn over the top card of each pile. (Naturally, they'll be the jack of hearts and the ten of clubs, the top two cards of the original deck.) Let's say your spectator turns over the ten of clubs first. Tell him that every card has a value and a suit and you're going to use the suit of this card. Then he'll turn over the other top card, the jack of hearts. Tell him that you'll use the value of this card, making your selection the jack of clubs. Turn over the predicted card to show your success.

I've devised a technique whereby you can make a wild stab in the dark at predicting a card your audience has just visualized without even seeing any cards. Just walk up to someone and ask her to think of a card. When she does, take an educated guess at what card she's chosen. If you miss, it's no big deal, just walk away. But if you hit, people will be convinced you have some crazy powers. You might think that you have only a one in fifty-two chance of nailing the card, but that's not correct.

I've found that when asked to think of a card, men will often come up with the ace of spades. Women's first choice is typically the queen of hearts. In order of popularity, men will answer ace, then seven, then four of spades. Women will guess queen, then ace, then seven of hearts. In general, when you say, "Think of any number from one to ten," 80 percent of people will respond, "Seven."

Now if your audience knows you're a magician or if you say, "Think of a card that I know you wouldn't normally think of," men might go with a seven of spades, women might change to an ace of hearts. You can also ask them to think of a "difficult" card. Saying "difficult" usually makes them think of the suit opposite the one they'd normally take. So men typically go to clubs, women to diamonds. If you ask a woman to think of a difficult card, she might come up with the seven of diamonds or, if she gets real tricky, the six of clubs, the six of spades, or the seven of either of those suits. If you ask a man to think of a difficult card, he'll usually say seven of spades, seven of clubs, six of spades, eight of spades, six of clubs, eight of clubs, three of spades, four of spades, or four of clubs, in that order. When you qualify your request with "difficult," neither men nor women will usually think of face cards or aces.

If you're afraid of failure, you can remove the top four most likely choices from the deck and place them in different pockets. Then ask the spectator to think of a card. If she names one of your

WOR 'N' END

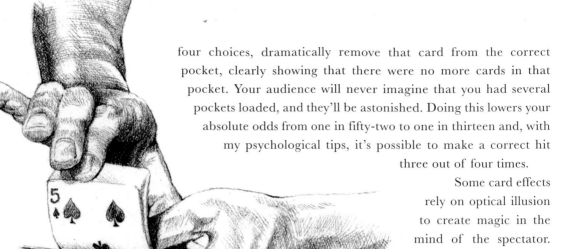

four choices, dramatically remove that card from the correct pocket, clearly showing that there were no more cards in that pocket. Your audience will never imagine that you had several pockets loaded, and they'll be astonished. Doing this lowers your absolute odds from one in fifty-two to one in thirteen and, with my psychological tips, it's possible to make a correct hit three out of four times.

Some card effects rely on optical illusion to create magic in the mind of the spectator. Back in the 1890s there was a mysterious Peruvian card magician who called himself L'Homme Masqué (the Masked Man). His real name was the Marquis d'Orighuala de Gago, and he performed many wondrous things with a deck of cards. Here's a variation on one of his best effects. Do a slow riffle of your deck of cards facing a spectator. Ask him to think of a card. Then hand the deck to him and have him shuffle it. After the shuffle, ask him to find the card he chose. Baffled, he won't be able to find the card in the deck. You then reach into his pocket and produce the king of clubs, which invariably is the card he selected.

Here's how this is done. Sometime before you do this effect, secretly slip the king of clubs into your spectator's pocket. Then, before you approach him, put the deck in a specific order: Put all the face cards, except the king of clubs (which you've already hidden) and the king of spades in the rear of the deck. At the front of the pack, you put the spades, with the ten of spades in the front. Behind that put a few hearts and diamonds (numerical cards only, no aces or face cards). Then put the following cards in this specific order: ten of clubs, nine of clubs, eight of clubs, king of spades, seven of clubs, six of clubs, five of clubs, four of clubs, three of clubs, two of clubs, and, finally, the ace of clubs. Then place the rest of the red cards, followed by the face cards.

Now you're going to "force" a card on your spectator by doing a slow riffle. Here's how. Hold the deck vertically in your left hand, as near the bottom as possible, your left thumb and first two fingers positioned as in Figure 4.2. Show the deck to your spectator so he

Fig. 4.2

can clearly see the bottom card. Ask him to think of any card he sees, but suggest a high card because that's more difficult. Then, using your right first finger, press down on the middle of the top edge of the cards and, using even pressure, move the finger from the front to the back of the deck, allowing the cards to flow evenly or riffle off the tip of your finger. Don't riffle the last quarter of the deck, because it will reveal more face cards. This should take about four seconds. Since the only face card in the beginning of the deck is the king of spades, that card will be forced into your spectator's mind.

Here's the wrinkle. Because of the placement of the king of spades in the middle of the clubs, the riffling effect will make the spectator believe that he's just seen the king of clubs. The slower the riffle, the more convincing this strobelike effect will be.

Now you're ready to complete the effect. Give your spectator the cards and make sure he shuffles them well, so their prearrangement is lost. Now when he looks for the king of clubs, which he thought he saw, he won't be able to find it. And when you direct him to look in his pocket and the king of clubs is there, you'll appear to have performed a miracle.

Here's another miraculous effect. This one, called Sound of the Voice, was devised by Charles Jordan, a Californian chicken farmer who invented great card effects. It also depends on prearranging a deck of cards. Take one entire suit of cards out of the deck. For our purposes, make it diamonds. Place six of the diamond cards on the top of the deck in any order. Put the remaining seven diamonds on the bottom of the deck. Now tell your spectator that you're going to do an effect that will blow her mind. Shuffle the deck, but make sure not to shuffle the bottom seven or the top six cards, so the diamonds remain on the top and bottom. Have your spectator deal the deck, one card at a time, into six piles, until she's dealt all the cards. So now, unbeknownst to your spectator, there's a diamond on the top and the bottom of each of the six piles, and two diamonds on top of one of them.

Now turn your back and have your spectator take a card out of the center of any of the six piles. Have her remember what card it is. Now instruct her to put the chosen card on top of any of the six piles and square each pile up. Tell her to pick up the piles of cards in any order make a full deck again, then give the deck a complete cut. Now tell her that just by the sound of her voice you can determine her selected card. Make up some story that subconsciously she

SHENT I.W.

Ace	Two	Three	Four	Five	Six	Seven	Eight	Nine	Ten	Jack	Queen	King

Fig. 4.3

will be bound to give you the card by the subtlest inflection of her voice. You can even tell her to try to disguise her voice.

Now have her deal one card at a time, face up, onto the table and name each card as it's dealt. If the first card is not a diamond and a diamond follows it, you know it's her card. It's more likely that the card will be buried somewhere other than on the top pile, so listen for diamonds. When you hear a diamond followed by another diamond, don't react, but if you hear a card that's between two diamonds, you'll know it was the chosen card. Let your spectator continue for a few more cards, then cut her off and tell her her chosen card. You'll always get it right.

All of these effects should astound any audience, but this next one may cause them to think you're Satan himself. Not only will you be able to say what card they chose from their own deck but you'll be able to do it over the phone. This is without doubt one of the finest card effects I've ever performed. Here's how it works.

Tell a friend to get a deck of cards and call you. After you get on the line, tell him to shuffle the deck. Now tell him to deal the cards face down into one pile, one at a time. Ask him to do it quietly so there's no way you can even hear over the phone how many cards he's dealt. He can deal as many cards as he wants, as long as it's less than half the deck. When he's ready, tell him to turn over the last card he dealt, remember it, and return it face down to the top of the pile.

Now, in order to help you get a mental image of that card, tell him to deal on top of that pile the number of cards that corresponds to the value of the chosen card. So, if his card was a three, he'd deal three more cards on top of it, if it was a nine, nine more cards. Jacks are eleven, queens are twelve, and kings are thirteen. Now tell him to pick up the pile he dealt and put it back on top of the deck he was dealing from so he has the whole deck in his hand.

While he was doing all this, you were preparing a piece of paper divided into thirteen columns, labeled ace, two, three, four, five, six, seven, eight, nine, ten, jack, queen, and king (see Figure 4.3). Now reiterate that there's absolutely no way you can know what your friend's card is. Okay, have him begin to deal the cards face up, one at a time, reading off each card. Remind him not to change the inflection of his voice when his card comes up. The first card he names is irrelevant, so don't bother to note it, but as he continues, make an entry for each card he names under your columns. So you enter the value and suit of the second card he names under your ace column. The third card gets cataloged under the two column, and so on.

Because you asked him to add the number of cards equal to the value of his chosen card to the top of his chosen card and you've thrown out the first card he named, you have to get a correspondence between his card and your column cards. For example, let's say his chosen card happened to be a three. So he added three cards on top of it. When he started to name the cards, you ignored the first one named, so his three card will fall into your three column. You now know that is potentially his card.

Sometimes by chance you get more than one match in your columns. Now you have to finesse your response. Let's say you have two potential hits—the two of diamonds and the queen of spades. Merely suggest that his card is a black card. If he says yes, then tell him it's the queen of spades. If he says no, you know it's the two of diamonds. If they were both, say, spades, suggest a high or a low card. After fishing for that innocuous answer, you've got your hit.

You can make this effect even more compelling. Tell your friend to begin to read off the cards, but as soon as he reads off the first card, interrupt him and tell him to cut the deck. Now you know the indifferent card that you would disregard anyway, so when he gets up to that card in his recitation, begin filling in your columns. You'll astound your audience even more now that he's cut his own deck.

I've done this effect to many people. One audience was a room full of ABC executives who called out their cards to me over a speakerphone while I was under the careful scrutiny of an impartial ABC employee, who accompanied me to an adjoining conference room. I knew I had nailed it when all the executives came running out of the office screaming. Moments later, we closed a deal for my first prime-time major-network TV special.

E.G. CELT

CHAPTER V
CONFIDENCE

*Careful attention to one thing
often proves superior to genius.*

—Cicero

Confidence

l Capone was in a good mood. He had just hustled his close friend Izzy Silverman out of ten thousand dollars by backing a young southern associate of Nick "the Greek" Dandolos, the legendary Chicago-based gambler, in an all-night poker game. Even better, near the end of the night, when a sleepy Silverman had finally passed out during a hand, Capone had had the lights in the room turned off and then had someone wake his friend up and tell him to play his hand. The darkness was punctuated by Izzy's plaintive cry, "Jesus, I've gone blind!" Capone roared with laughter.

The game broke up, and Capone, Nick the Greek, and his southern friend went to get some breakfast. Capone was still chuckling over his practical joke when he stopped at a fruit stand and bought everyone oranges. Always a gambler, he offered to bet Nick the Greek's friend that he couldn't throw the orange over the top of the building across the street. Nick's friend replied that if he could go back and pick out a little-less-ripe orange, he'd be happy to bet Capone five hundred dollars even up that he could do it. "Go get an orange," Capone said with a smile.

Seconds later the young southerner was back. He took a deep breath and a running start, and hurled the fruit. It easily cleared the roof of the building. Capone was impressed as he handed the man five hundred dollars cash. He would have been a lot less impressed (and in a much worse mood) if he'd learned that when the southerner went back to the fruit stand he exchanged his orange for a lemon. Harder and smaller, the lemon was much easier to throw that distance.

The man who had the guts to con Al Capone (and lived to tell the tale) was one of the greatest hustlers of all time. He was a master of the short con (taking a sucker's money without an elaborate, time-consuming sting), making a ton of money with his proposition betting. He was born Alvin Clarence Thomas, but he was known all across America, from every golf course to

every illegal high-stakes card game, as Titanic Thompson.

Legend had it that Titanic received his nickname because he dressed up in women's clothes and escaped in a rowboat designated for women and children as the famed ocean liner was slowly sinking. That wasn't exactly true. He was nicknamed Titanic by a gambler in Joplin, Missouri, who, when asked the name of the young guy who was beating everyone, said, "I don't know. But it ought to be Titanic the way he's sinking everyone here."

Gambling was in Titanic's blood. He was born in tiny Rogers,

Arkansas, on November 30, 1892, but his father, an inveterate poker player, refused to interrupt his card game to be at his wife's side for the delivery. He saw his son for the first time two days later. Five months later his father left the house for good, but the branch didn't fall far from the tree.

Titanic was only eleven when he worked his first scam. He lived in the country, near the White River, and all that summer he watched with envy as the "rich" townsfolk from Rogers came to fish with the finest gear the local hardware store offered. His cane pole paled in comparison. After watching one tourist with a particularly nice rod and reel, Ti put his plan into action.

He had already trained his dog to fetch, even to retrieve objects that had been thrown in the water. So one morning Ti left home with his dog, his cane pole, and his trusty .22 rifle. He staked out a spot close to where his mark had been regularly fishing. Sure enough, the man showed up and cast his rod. The young boy wandered over and struck up a conversation, all the while casually throwing a stick into the water and commanding the dog to fetch it.

Ti innocently told the city slicker that his pet had an amazing ability to retrieve things and bragged that the animal could even fetch a rock from the bottom of the river. The man found that hard to believe, and the two agreed to a bet. Since he had no money, Titanic proposed betting his dog against the guy's fishing rod. The guy agreed, but first he suggested that they mark the rock so they'd be sure the dog retrieved the same rock. Thompson nodded, marked a rock with an *X*, and threw it into the stream. The dog returned with a rock between his teeth. It was marked with the *X*.

The man was amazed, but when Ti asked for his rod, the man laughed the kid off. He wasn't about to hand over his brandnew, expensive rod to some fool kid. That was where the .22 came in. Ti aimed it right at the city slicker's head. Seconds later, Titanic had his new rod. What the man didn't know was that Titanic probably also had a sore arm from spending the entire previous day marking thousands of rocks with *X*'s and throwing them into that watering hole.

By age nineteen, Titanic had learned almost every card con imaginable. Years later he would fool Houdini with his ability to palm cards. Ti was also a great pool shark, an expert card tosser, and an amazing horseshoe player. He knew that to win at gambling, you had to use every edge imaginable. In Minneapolis he challenged Frank Jackson, the world champion horseshoe pitcher, to a match. Of course, he also made side bets on the competition. Then, unbeknownst to Jackson, Titanic set up a court that was forty-one feet long, instead of the regulation forty. Ti had spent months practicing at the slightly longer distance. By the time Jackson could compensate for the extra foot, Titanic had an insurmountable lead, and he walked away with over two thousand dollars.

Titanic was a genius when it came to scams. In addition to possessing amazing athletic ability and hand-eye coordination that was second to none, Titanic hardly ever lost a bet. Just before he turned thirty he tired of all-night, smoke-filled poker games and took up golf to get some fresh air and sunshine. Within a few years he was probably the greatest amateur golfer ever. Of course, he used his skills to begin fleecing rich country clubbers by betting on golf rounds. He'd typically throw the first game, get them to bet more heavily on the second game, then handily beat the suckers. Then he'd entice his marks to play another round for even more money, only this time he'd shoot lefty. What Titanic never told his opponents was that he was a natural lefty.

Titanic once hustled a stronger, younger golf pro and got the guy to accept a match at a grand a hole. What's more, Titanic generously offered to allow the pro to take three drives off each tee and count the best one. The pro was up seven thousand dollars after the first seven holes, but suddenly he began to blow easy shots, and Titanic won the last eleven straight holes and pocketed four grand. By the eighteenth hole, the pro realized why his game had fallen apart—he was incredibly arm weary from driving three times on every hole.

Marlon Brando's character in Guys and Dolls, Sky Masterson, *was modeled on Titanic.*

Titanic was best known for his crazy proposition bets. He'd be driving along with a few friends, and they'd see a highway sign, JOPLIN—20 MILES. Suddenly Titanic would stop the car. "There's no way that it's twenty miles to town. I know distance, and it ain't that far." Pretty soon he'd have five hundred dollars' worth of bets lined up, and they'd proceed to town, watching the odometer. Sure enough, it was fifteen miles to the town line, and Titanic won the five hundred dollars. It was an unfair contest, though.

The day before, Titanic had dug up the sign and moved it five miles closer to town.

Titanic often bet unsuspecting marks that he could hurl a walnut over a building; then he'd employ sleight of hand and switch the real walnut for one that had been filled with lead pellets. He did the same thing at a Yankees game; he beat the guy sitting next to him out of a hundred dollars when he bet that he could hurl a peanut past the pitcher's mound. His weighted peanut almost beaned the center fielder.

Ti also ran some unmerciful scams on the New York mobster Arnold Rothstein. One time he bet Rothstein that the next car from

The Hundred-dollar-bill bar scam

Even though he wasn't a magician, Titanic Thompson employed the skills magicians use when they set up their audiences for the kill. The psychology of a con is very similar to the psychology of magic. Sometimes the lines regrettably blur, as is the case with this famous scam, which has been run on unsuspecting bartenders for many years. It takes a fair degree of sleight-of-hand skill, and it winds up costing the poor bartender about ninety-five dollars when his register comes up short, so I don't advocate actually doing this.

Go into a bar accompanied by a confederate. The place must be busy. There also have to be two bartenders on duty, and they have to share the same cash register. You go to one end of the bar and strike up a conversation with someone who's drinking there. Maybe you do a simple card effect or two. The bartender comes over and watches. Then say you've got something you want to show them. Tell them that you can make a hundred-dollar bill disappear and reappear somewhere else. Take out a hundred and, just to authenticate the bill, have the bartender sign his name on the back of it with a pen. (It's imperative that it's on the back of the bill.)

Here's where the sleight of hand comes in. Take the bill back, fold it up, and make it vanish. You secretly hand it off to your confederate, who's standing behind you. As soon as he gets the bill, he walks to the other end of the bar and orders a drink. He pays for the drink with the signed hundred-dollar bill, but he hands it face side up to the other bartender. In a crowded bar, the other bartender will give it a cursory

New Jersey that turned the corner would have three 3's on its license plate. Sure enough, it did. Of course it did: Titanic had hired a cab-driver to drive the car around the corner right at that time. Rothstein plotted revenge. A few gamblers would take the train every day from Manhattan to the racetrack. Each day they'd put fifty dollars in a pool and bet how many white horses they'd see on the ride out. One day Rothstein picked an unusually high number. He was stunned when Titanic picked an even *higher* number. Rothstein had rented some white horses and set them up along the route to inflate the numbers and win the bet, but Titanic went one step further. Rothstein was beside himself when he looked out the train window

look, immediately put it in the register, and give your confederate the change.

Meanwhile, you've been making passes with your hands. Then you open them and show your empty hands to the original bartender and anyone else who's watching. Now tell the bartender that, even though it seems impossible, you've made the hundred-dollar bill reappear in the register. He goes to the register, roots around, and finds the bill he signed. Amazed, he returns it to you. Now you've got your original hundred, at least ninety-five dollars in change, and your friend got a free drink. You just have to make sure that you don't do this in a place you frequent, because at the end of the night, the bartenders will be looking for that missing cash.

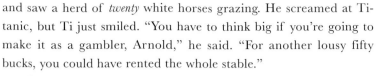

P. T. Barnum. Innovative, nervy, audacious—somewhat typical of New Englanders.

and saw a herd of *twenty* white horses grazing. He screamed at Titanic, but Ti just smiled. "You have to think big if you're going to make it as a gambler, Arnold," he said. "For another lousy fifty bucks, you could have rented the whole stable."

One winter in Chicago, Titanic came up with his most famous scam. He had been hanging around a municipal golf course clubhouse, hustling hard. After bragging about how great he was at golf, he offered to bet anyone that he could drive a ball at least five hundred yards. The only condition was he got to pick the course and the hole. Within minutes he had a couple of grand in action, and the gamblers were off to a course on the outskirts of town. They followed Titanic to the fifth hole. "Look, since I got to hit the ball so far, I don't know if I can keep it on the fairway. Is that all right?" Titanic asked. The guys all agreed.

Titanic teed up his ball, then suddenly turned ninety degrees to one side and walloped a drive that landed square in the center of a huge frozen lake that abutted the golf course. The ball was probably still skidding across the ice as Titanic drove back to Chicago, thousands of dollars richer.

Titanic Thompson spent his whole life crisscrossing America, looking for new marks. He won almost a quarter of a million dollars hustling Arnold Rothstein in a rigged card game in New York. When Rothstein was reluctant to pay up, he was accidentally shot and killed by one of the card players. Titanic became an instant celebrity while testifying for the government at the trial of the man who fatally wounded Rothstein. Of course, he testified with a straight face that it would have been impossible to rig a game like that. Even before the trial, Titanic had become regular fodder for the gossip columns. Damon Runyon modeled Sky Masterson, the womanizing character from his play *Guys and Dolls*, on Thompson. Marlon Brando played him in the movie.

Celebrity is the last thing a scammer needs. After the Rothstein murder trial, Titanic left New York to hustle golf games and speculate in oil rights. By the end of his life, Titanic had scammed, hustled, and ultimately burned through millions of dollars. He was married five times, not once to a woman older than twenty. He also killed five times, but each time it was ruled self-defense. He finally died in a rest home in Texas at eighty-two years old. In his room they found cartons and cartons of cigarettes that he had won by hustling his geriatric housemates in card games and horseshoe matches. The funny thing was, Titanic Thompson never smoked.

Although I appreciated a good short con, people who took the time to devise elaborate hoaxes really fascinated me. One of the most creative hoaxers of all time was also the man who invented the modern-day notion of show business. Phineas Taylor Barnum was born on July 5, 1810, in Bethel, Connecticut. His father was a grocer and, after trying his hand at owning a fruit store, editing a liberal weekly newspaper, conducting legal lotteries, and selling hats, the then twenty-five-year-old Barnum reverted to the family trade and opened a small grocery store in New York. One day one of his customers came into the store and changed the course of American entertainment history. He told Barnum that his friend R. W. Lindsay owned a slave woman named Joice Heth who was 161 years old and claimed to have been George Washington's nurse. She had been exhibited in Philadelphia, but Lindsay, fearing that he wasn't cut out for show business, was looking to sell his attraction.

Barnum rushed to Philadelphia, met with Heth, marveled at her anecdotes about our first president, obtained documentation allegedly verifying her age, and purchased her (bargaining Lindsay down from three thousand dollars to one thousand in the process). He rented a hall in New York, began a massive advertising campaign, and displayed Heth. She would sit onstage and weep as she recalled moving anecdotes about little Georgie. She'd also answer questions from the audience and sing gospel songs. She was such a hit that Barnum was soon grossing fifteen hundred dollars a week. After several months in New York, he took Heth on the road, where he repeated his success.

In Boston, after interest in the allegedly oldest woman in the world began to fade, Barnum came up with a brainstorm. He wrote an anonymous letter to a local paper claiming, "Joice Heth is not a human being. What purports to be a remarkably old woman is simply a curiously constructed automaton, made up of whalebone, India-rubber, and numberless springs, ingeniously put together." Thousands flocked back to see if Joice Heth was really real.

Fidel Castro made better use of doves than any magician to this day. When he spoke to his supporters at his first triumphant rally, trained doves were released from amid the crowd. When one of the doves landed on his shoulder, the Cuban people perceived it as a sign from above that he was ordained to be their savior.

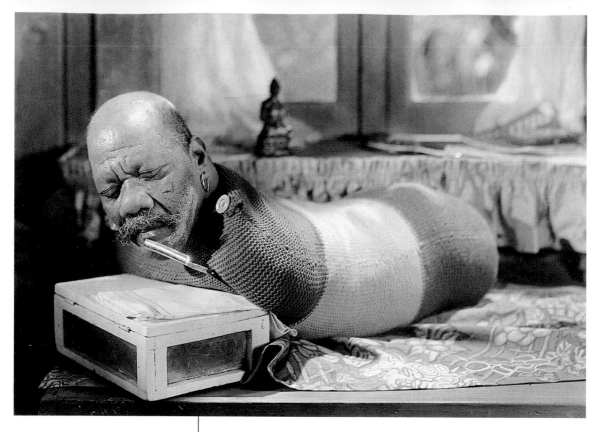

Randian, the famous living torso, in a still from the 1931 movie Freaks

Barnum exhibited Heth until she was too ill to appear in public. After her death, he gained even more publicity by allowing her body to be autopsied. When the medical procedure revealed that Heth was at best only eighty years old, Barnum leaked a story to the press that the autopsy itself was a hoax, and the dead dissected woman was actually "Aunt Nelly" of Harlem. The entire Joice Heth affair made Barnum the most famous promoter of his era.

Hoaxing and humbugging came naturally to Barnum. His maternal grandfather, Phineas Taylor, was a lifelong practical jokester. In fact, when P.T. was christened, Taylor gave him a gift of five acres of land in Connecticut called Ivy Island. During his childhood his entire family reminded Barnum that he was the richest child in town, being the beneficiary of such valuable property. Finally, when he was ten years old, P.T. begged to see his dream island. One day he and his father set off for the promised land. After hours of trudging through muddy swamps and creeks, they finally reached his treasured domain, but young Barnum was incredulous. "I saw nothing but a few stunted ivies and straggling trees," he later wrote. "The truth flashed on me. I had been the laughingstock of the family and neighborhood for years. My valuable 'Ivy Island' was an almost inaccessible, worthless bit of barren land." His grandfather's protracted practical joke was a valuable lesson to the future entrepreneur. He wouldn't be fooled again; in fact, he spent the rest of his life fooling others, for fun and profit.

By 1842 Barnum had opened the American Museum, a vast dime museum in New York City. He took out full-page ads (one commentator called him the Shakespeare of advertising) and festooned the museum with bright lights and colorful banners. He hired a band of the worst musicians he could find and had them serenade the passersby from the balcony. Their inharmonious music was meant to drive people off the street and directly into the museum. "Of course, the music was poor," Barnum wrote. "When people expect to get 'something for nothing' they are sure to be cheated."

Once inside, patrons could see, according to Barnum, "industrious fleas, automatons, jugglers, ventriloquists, living statuary, gypsies, albinos, fat boys, giants, dwarfs, rope-dancers, dioramas, panoramas, knitting machines, American Indians." The variety was endless and the turnover frequent.

Barnum continually pulled the wool over people's eyes. He advertised "The Great Model of Niagara Falls, With Real Water!" The public streamed into the exhibit and were stunned to see an eighteen-inch replica of the falls and the surrounding area, built to scale. After a huge publicity buildup, Barnum exhibited what was purported to be an authentic mermaid fossil from the "Feejee" Islands. Years later he would admit the mermaid was a hoax, having been made by combining the upper body of a monkey with the lower half of a fish.

When crowds lingered too long in his museum, preventing new paying customers from entering, Barnum came up with an ingenious solution. He had a worker paint a four-foot-square canvas and proudly displayed it over a rear exit door that was hardly ever used. It read THIS WAY TO THE EGRESS. Figuring that they were about to see some startling new species of the animal kingdom, the crowds bustled out the door and found themselves in a back alley, locked out of the museum.

Because he was the king of humbugs, it's easy to believe that Barnum actually uttered the quote most often attributed to him—"There's a sucker born every minute." In reality, though, he never said it. When Barnum tried to buy the rights to a phony "primitive" giant, the original exhibitors refused him, so P.T. just commissioned

his own fake giant and claimed that *his* giant was the genuine one. David Hannum, one of the owners of the original fake, described the masses who flocked to Barnum's exhibit as the infamous suckers who were born every minute. Of course, it wasn't far from the truth. Barnum *did* say "the American public likes to be humbugged," and he spent the rest of his life proving that maxim true for all nationalities.

Ingenious hoaxes might have made Barnum's reputation, but he proved to be able to channel his incredible showmanship into legitimate ventures as well. He made a fortune promoting the American concerts of Jenny Lind, an amazing singer who was known as the Swedish Nightingale. He created the three-ring circus and, in partnership with James Bailey, made it a national treasure. Still, he never could resist a good humbug. He made millions displaying Tom Thumb, a midget who thrilled audiences by dressing up in outlandish costumes and reciting corny, pun-filled patter. He made even more money by exhibiting both Tom Thumb and his midget wife, Lavinia. When interest in the two flagged, Barnum acquired an orphan and, claiming that the Thumbs had a son, exhibited the midget family. After the child outgrew its "parents," Barnum was forced to rent a local baby in every country the Thumbs visited.

Even during his later circus days, the old humbugger surfaced. Every year the circus would feature one new blockbuster act. In 1880 Barnum showcased

Waino and Plutano, Barnum's Wild Men of Borneo, weren't really from Borneo.

the Wild Men of Borneo, a pair of longhaired, muscular dwarfs "so wild and ferocious . . . they could easily subdue tigers." The Bornean Wild Men became one of the most famous freak acts in the world, earning over $200,000 in their lifetimes, but they were neither wild nor from Borneo. They were retarded brothers who lived on a farm in Ohio.

Despite all the humbugs, Barnum grew to be a cherished American icon. By the end of his life, he had become a model of respectability, even winning election as mayor of Bridgeport, Connecticut, but he was always remembered as the self-appointed Prince of Humbugs, and he delighted in that crown, as he must have delighted in this description of him in *Yankee Doodle*, attributed to

Herman Melville: "If the whole world of animated nature—human or brute—at any time produces a monstrosity or a wonder, she has but one object in view—to benefit BARNUM. BARNUM, under the happy influence of a tallow candle in some corner or other of Yankee land, was born sole heir to all her lean men, fat women, dwarfs, two-headed cows, amphibious sea-maidens, large-eyed owls, small-eyed mice, rabbit-eating anacondas, bugs, monkeys and mummies."

It was someone other than Barnum, however, who perpetrated the most famous hoax in American history, although it was hardly even a hoax. Orson Welles was only twenty-three in 1938, when he directed and starred in a weekly radio show for the CBS network called *The Mercury Theatre on the Air*. Even though he produced quality radio drama, he'd typically get trounced in the ratings by the ventriloquist-comedian Edgar Bergen and his wooden dummy, Charlie McCarthy. The night before Halloween 1938, Welles was set to air a dramatic adaptation by Howard Koch of the 1898 sci-fi masterpiece *The War of the Worlds*, written by the Englishman H. G. Wells. Welles's colleagues warned him against doing the show, maintaining that a radio drama in which Martians battled Earthlings for the future of the planet was just too unbelievable.

Welles didn't care. He went ahead with the broadcast, which took the form of a radio station interrupting their programming with live bulletins from the scene of the "invasion." To make it more compelling, Welles and Koch transformed H. G. Wells's invasion of England into an attack on a sleepy town in New Jersey called Grovers Mill. A CBS announcer clearly introduced the show as "Orson Welles and the Mercury Theatre on the Air in *War of the Worlds* by H. G. Wells." Then Welles set the stage with introductory remarks that clearly set the program one year in the future.

The introduction over, the play faded in on an announcer in the middle of a weather report. The small core audience of *The Mercury Theatre* heard this setup and realized the fictional context of what was to follow, but what Welles probably didn't anticipate was that a vast majority of loyal Charlie McCarthy fans would get bored with their show when, at precisely 8:12 P.M., the comedy gave way to a musical segment. All across America listeners began to radio-station surf. When they came upon CBS, they were startled to hear a dra-

Johnny Eck, the reason Rajah Raboid was able to do his legendary sawing illusion. For more details, see Ricky Jay's book Learned Pigs & Fireproof Women.

Howard Hughes was the second man to fly solo around the world. He did it in half the time it took Charles Lindbergh, the first to achieve this feat. At the same time that he was breaking aviation records, he owned RKO studios and produced the classic film _Citizen Kane_.

TIME

THE WEEKLY NEWS-MAGAZINE

HOWARD HUGHES

"Well, all I can say is that this crowd has frightened me more than anything in the past three days."
—Upon facing the crowd in Brooklyn's Floyd Bennett Field on July 14, 1938, after his record-breaking flight around the world.

Hughes dated some of the most beautiful actresses of his time, including Ava Gardner, Jean Harlow, Marilyn Monroe, and Bette Davis. He was one of America's first self-made billionaires and later became the world's most famous recluse.

matic announcement couched as a bulletin breaking into the dance music of Ramon Raquello and his orchestra, in which it was stated that a "huge, flaming object, believed to be a meteorite, fell on a farm in the neighborhood of Grovers Mill, New Jersey."

Following a return to the swing band, a commentator named Carl Phillips interrupted the music again to file a live report from the scene of the crash. In excited tones he declared that the debris from space was not a meteorite but a huge cylindrical object. After conducting interviews with bystanders, he went on to describe a being emerging from the top of the object.

Phillips's next report was cut short when the creature began shooting a heat ray at the onlookers. Then the radio announcer turned the microphone over to the commander of the state militia, who declared martial law. Troops were rushed to the area. It was reported that the charred body of the reporter, Phillips, had been recovered. Finally, another announcer's voice was heard pronouncing that the creatures were "the vanguard of an invading army from the planet Mars."

More Martian machines were reported to have landed across the country, spewing lethal black gas. The invaders crossed the Passaic River into the Jersey marshes. Another machine straddled the Pulaski Skyway, heading toward Manhattan. Chaos reigned. The army and air force proved ineffectual against the invaders. After broadcasting live reports from the field of action, a CBS announcer in New York City took the microphone and declared that all resources had been useless against the invaders.

The station went dead. After an attempt by another station to communicate with the New York announcer failed, there was a break and, for the first time since the beginning of the show, a CBS announcer came on to remind the audience that they'd been listening to an original dramatization of *War of the Worlds*. But it was too little too late; pandemonium had already broken out all across America. Bus terminals in Manhattan filled with panicked passengers who wanted to go anywhere as long as it was away from the Martians. Terrified New Jersey residents caused traffic jams as they piled their belongings into their cars and prepared to flee. People flocked to churches to pray. Others jammed hospital emergency rooms; a few even had heart attacks. People organized makeshift militias, ready to do battle with their otherworldly foes. In Pittsburgh a man came home to find his wife on the verge of swallowing

poison—"I'd rather die this way," she sobbed. On a college campus in the Southwest, coeds wept and comforted each other and called home to say good-bye to their parents for the last time. Welles, who was a great amateur magician, had created the ultimate illusion—live coverage of the War of the Worlds.

If the panicked listeners had bothered to stay tuned to the rest of the program, they would have heard a poignant monologue from a character who somehow survived the invasion and reported from the streets of now deserted Manhattan that the Martian invasion ultimately failed when the interplanetary storm troopers all collapsed and died in Central Park—the victims of good old Earthling germs. They would also have heard the young director directly address his six million listeners, informing them that this was "the Mercury Theatre's own radio version of dressing up in a sheet and jumping out of a bush and saying Boo!"

As soon as the show was over, the CBS switchboard was flooded with irate callers. Welles and his cast snuck out the back of the studio to avoid the reporters and police who had been banging on the front door. (Even during the show, a CBS executive had pleaded with Welles to break into the program and allay the fears of frightened listeners. "They're scared? Good! They're supposed to be scared," Welles told him.)

The New York Times.

Copyright, 1938, by The New York Times Company.

NEW YORK, MONDAY, OCTOBER 31, 1938.

MEAD STANDS PAT AS A NEW DEALER IN BID FOR SENATE

Democratic Candidate Opposes Any Except Minor Changes in Labor and Security Laws

UPHOLDS THEORY OF TVA

Radio Listeners in Panic, Taking War Drama as Fact

Many Flee Homes to Escape 'Gas Raid From Mars'—Phone Calls Swamp Police at Broadcast of Wells Fantasy

A wave of mass hysteria seized thousands of radio listeners throughout the nation between 8:15 and 9:30 o'clock last night when a broadcast of a dramatization of H. G. Wells's fantasy, "The War of the Worlds," led thousands to

OUSTED JEWS FIND REFUGE IN POLAND AFTER BORDER STAY

Exiles Go to Relatives' Homes or to Camps Maintained by Distribution Committee

REVEAL CRUELTY OF TRIP

San Francisco Chronicle

THE CITY'S ONLY HOME-OWNED NEWSPAPER

SAN FRANCISCO, MONDAY, OCTOBER 31, 1938.   DAILY 5 CENTS, SUNDAY 10 CENTS

Probe Feud Dies Charges New Deal Intimidation

Rail Wages F. R. Meets Employers, Labor Today

U. S. Terrorized By Radio's 'Men From Mars'

DAILY NEWS   FINAL

FAKE RADIO 'WAR' STIRS TERROR THROUGH U.S.

"War" Victim

"I Didn't Know".

The next day, after *The New York Times*'s front page blared RADIO LISTENERS IN PANIC, TAKING WAR DRAMA AS FACT. MANY FLEE HOMES TO ESCAPE "GAS RAID FROM MARS"—PHONE CALLS SWAMP POLICE, Welles appeared more contrite. He issued a statement claiming he was "deeply regretful to learn that the H. G. Wells fantasy . . . which was designed as entertainment, has caused some apprehension among Columbia network listeners. Far from expecting the radio audience to take the program as fact rather than as a fictional presentation, we feared the classic H. G. Wells story . . . might appear too old fashioned for public consumption." He later told the *Times*, "I don't think we will choose anything like this again."

Despite Welles's statement, the fallout continued. One midwestern mayor whose streets had been clogged with frightened mobs threatened to come to New York and personally "punch Orson Welles in the nose." CBS apologized to the nation. The FCC held hearings and labeled the broadcast "regrettable." Some people even filed lawsuits, but they were thrown out of court since there had been announcements during the show that what was being broadcast was fiction. In the end most of the frightened listeners were left with egg on their faces, but Welles wound up with some very valuable soup on his, as Campbell's soups,

Orson Welles scared the nation during his live broadcast of The Mercury Theatre on the Air *in 1938.*

thrilled with the notoriety, signed on to be the new major sponsor of the show.

The story didn't end there. In February 1949 an enterprising radio station in Quito, Ecuador, decided to do their own version of an alien invasion. Again, panicked listeners fled into the streets. This time, when they found out that the broadcast was a fictional enactment, the enraged mob surrounded the local newspaper building, where the radio station had its offices. Windows were shattered, fires were started, and the police were attacked. Before the military could restore order, six people had been killed, fifteen had been injured, and the fires had decimated the entire building.

When I was eleven years old, my mother got remarried and we moved to New Jersey. There's not much to say about my growing up in Jersey, except that Jersey was where Orson Welles set his remarkable hoax. I spent a lot of time alone working on my magic. I'd practice for at least eight hours a day, every day. If we were eating dinner, my hands would be under the table working on some manipulation. Even though I was always practicing, I never performed magic for any of my peers because I didn't think they'd appreciate it.

I did do some strange things growing up. On my way home from school, if I'd pass by a huge tree I'd convince myself that if I didn't leap up and rip a leaf off the highest branch, I'd come down with the latest horrible disease I had learned about in health class. I had to get home faster than the bus, or grab the leaf, or walk in a certain line; otherwise I'd be doomed.

On top of these compulsions, I just enjoyed testing the limits of my endurance. My friends and I would go punch for punch, and no matter how much I hurt, I never let on. We'd be swimming and have competitions to see who could hold his breath for the longest time while underwater. The others would hold their breath, then cheat some air and go down again. They'd do this three or four times; meanwhile, I was underwater the whole time. I bet that I could do five laps swimming underwater. I collected five hundred dollars, but I came out with purple lips and gasping for air.

I did other daredevil stunts. My friends and I would walk across a local bridge that was hundreds of feet

above a shallow river. Without thinking, I'd jump on top of the skinny ledge and walk across, precariously balancing myself. The people in the cars that passed would honk their horns and scream at me to get down, but I didn't care. On the outskirts of town, there was a formation of high cliffs that I'd always be climbing. One day I lost my footing and fell down a huge cliff, rolling and tumbling the whole way. When I finally stopped moving, I got up and dusted myself off. I didn't have even one scratch. My friends nicknamed me the Cat after that fall.

I guess I did other unusual things, although to me at the time they didn't seem too strange. I slept on the hardwood floor of my bedroom for a whole year because I was convinced that there were mites in my bed. My best friend, Jim Eisele, remembers that when we were in junior high I stayed in my closet for nearly two days. I don't remember this, but I guess I had some issues and that was my way of resolving them. Jim says my mom even brought my food to the closet and I ate it in there. She was always supportive of me, no matter what I did.

My mom gave me so much confidence I just knew that, when I was creating magic, there were no limits to where it could take me. I was positive that I could get anything I wanted. It was all about a serious application of will. I knew this when I was sixteen years old. That year I borrowed a friend's Super 8 camera and made a tape. On the tape my friend pretended that he was interviewing me. I went overboard and made up the craziest, most outrageous fantasies I could imagine. I told him Spike Lee was going to make some commercials for my first television special. I also mentioned that I was doing a film for De Niro's company and that I would be doing my magic all over the world. Within years all of that had come true.

(above, left to right)
Welles as Citizen Kane, Macbeth, and himself. Orson was also a magician.

CHAPTER VI
PLAYING THE PART OF A MAGICIAN

I began revolution with eighty-two men. If I had [to] do it again, I do it with ten or fifteen and absolute faith. It does not matter how small you are if you have faith and plan of action.

—Fidel Castro

Playing the Part of a Magician

Ideas come from strange places. One morning I was running late for my acting class. I rushed into the subway and saw the train pulling into the station, so I just hopped the turnstile. Unfortunately, the Transit Police were doing a sweep that day, and I was brought into a holding cell and ordered to appear in court at a later date. That date just happened to fall on my last day of classes. I figured that I would be the first to arrive in court, pay my fine, and still make it to school. But the wheels of justice spin slowly, so after a few hours of sitting on those wonderful wood benches, I decided to go to school, say my good-byes, and then come back and clear up my case. After I left the courtroom, a woman who had been sitting next to me discovered that money had been stolen from her purse. The thieves were a sketchy couple who had been sitting on her other side. Apparently they blamed the heist on me, so when I returned, four policemen pulled me out of the courtroom, strip-searched me, and escorted me to Central Booking.

I felt like I was in the middle of a Kafka novel. Since it was a Friday afternoon, there was no chance that I could straighten this out until Monday at the earliest. So I was facing seventy-two hours in a big holding cell where over thirty hardened criminals were congregated in one small cell while they awaited their court appearances. As an eighteen-year-old turnstile jumper, I knew that being the least threatening guy in the cell was not a good thing. So I looked around and saw four brothers—the biggest, toughest guys in the place—sitting in the center of the cell playing a card game called Spades. I

TAKE FIVE: Spike Lee directs pal David Blaine last week. The New York street magician once terrified David Geffen by "levitating" 6 inches off the ground with out saying he was an illusionist.

http://www.mostnewyork.com

walked right up to them and grabbed their deck of cards.

"What's up with you, man?" the scariest-looking guy snarled.

"You know the three-card-monte hustle?" I asked. "I can show you how to do it, but better."

I started doing magic to them.

I did a variation of three-card monte and floored them. Then I had one of them choose a card, but not trusting me, he put the card back in the deck and shuffled it. I responded by taking the deck and throwing it up at the ceiling. All the cards came fluttering down over our heads, but one card stuck to the ceiling. It was his card—the four of spades. By now everybody in the cell had congregated around us. Then I did some crazy card effects, and the whole cellblock went wild. I was getting high-fived right and left; people were offering me cigarettes and sharing the mustard that they used to spice up the standard-issue bologna sandwiches we were fed. Their reactions to the magic were so animated and intense I instantly realized that this is what magic on television should be— magic done to real people in real places.

Me, eighteen years old, doing magic to Jack Nicholson in Saint-Tropez

Around that time I became interested in Orson Welles, who, besides being an amazing filmmaker, was also a magician. In his documentary *F Is for Fake,* Welles quotes Robert-Houdin, who wrote, "A magician is an actor playing the part of a magician." That made instinctive sense to me. While most people's image of a magician is that of someone who walks up to you and pulls quarters out of your ears, I sensed that magic, at its best, could be an intense and emotional experience—not just a series of amusing little "tricks."

It seemed to me that showmen like Harry Houdini and Uri Geller understood that. They didn't even refer to themselves as magicians, because they didn't want to be associated with petty trickery. Houdini called himself a "mystifier" or an "escape artist." Uri Geller referred to himself as a "paranormalist." What they had in common was the innovative way they presented magic, so that they captivated the world's imagination and led their audiences to believe that it was okay to believe.

Just as I was beginning to apply these ideas to my own magic, my world suddenly took a very unexpected and, I felt, undeserved turn—my mom's cancer, which had been in remission, returned. The doctors warned her that unless she immediately resumed chemotherapy and radiation treatments, she'd have only months to live. She did resume treatment, but it was almost as bad as the disease, so after doing some research, she decided to fight the cancer her own way—by adopting a strict macrobiotic diet of pure, organic foods that had no preservatives or chemicals. She also refused to allow the disease to redefine her life, so she continued to teach underprivileged kids, study spirituality, and treat each person she met with the same respect and dignity—no matter what their class, color, or status. After she followed her own regimen for a few months, a miracle happened: the tumors stopped growing and even began to recede. The doctors couldn't explain it.

My mom's illness made me grow up fast. I felt as if her sickness had thrown me into a cold world with nothing. When you're faced with a fear so great, you realize how trivial all of your other concerns really are. It's a very strong awakening. Her illness became the central focus of my life. I got a job waiting tables at a macrobiotic restaurant downtown, so I could learn how to cook for her.

The restaurant gave me a unique stage on which to work my art. Health food restaurants attract an incredibly diverse group of spiritually inclined people, in search of the miraculous and more open

than most to a sense of wonder and enchantment. So I applied some of the lessons I had learned in acting school and created a character—a waiter with special powers. I cultivated an aura of mystery. First of all, nobody could understand why this strange, dark-skinned kid was working there—a really small restaurant where the rest of the staff was Japanese. To add to the strangeness, I'd do things like take my customers' checks and surreptitiously Scotch-tape them to my back. When someone finished their meal and looked like they were about to ask for their check, I'd rush over, stare intently at them, reach around to my back, pull their check off, and solemnly hand it to them, as if I were an insane person. That really threw people for a loop. And when they'd offer me hundred-percent tips, I'd just hand them the tip back and tell them that I wasn't doing this for the money, which confused them even more.

I'd routinely practice my sleight of hand on the patrons. For instance, take this simple card switch: I'd show a customer a card, then sandwich it between her hands. Then I'd show her that her card was now in the deck, and when she turned over the card in her hands, it had miraculously changed to another card. One evening I did this effect to a man who was dining there alone. He was so astounded by the switch that he became convinced that I had actually stopped time, pulled the card out of this hand, put the other card in its place, put his hands back together, and then restarted time. He was still in awe when he left the restaurant. I finished my shift a few hours later and walked to the Little Italy apartment where I was living, sleeping on a friend's couch. It was at least fifteen blocks from the restaurant, but just as I was about to enter my building, I recognized the man I had waited on earlier that evening. He came up to me and admitted

With Michael Jackson, the King of Pop, and Uri Geller (second from right), two forces of magic, in London, June 2002

HE, ALOST

On **Oprah**, *early in my career*

that he had been lurking outside the restaurant for hours till I left, and then had followed me home. "You have to tell me," he implored. "How did you get that card out of my hand?" The lesson wasn't lost on me. If I could make the restaurant clientele believe in my magic, I could probably make others into believers, too.

Now that my mom was doing better, I began to spend more time in Manhattan. Around that time, I met the owner of Tatou, and he offered me a chance to do magic for the patrons of his trendy restaurant/club. I wouldn't get a salary, but on an average night, I could make a few hundred dollars in tips.

Doing magic in a restaurant was tough, and helped me build my chops quickly. The first rule I learned was that when you walk up to a group of people who are sitting down, they initially don't want you anywhere near them. It's imposing enough to have a waiter standing over you, let alone a magician. So I devised a strategy. I'd target the person who was most likely to be paying the bill (or the woman who seemed to be getting the most attention at the table). It wasn't a question of *if* I could win them over; I never gave them a choice. I would usually do my strongest piece of magic right off the bat—something that was very visual but also could be done in less than thirty seconds. This was to capture their attention. After a few months and much experimentation, I fine-tuned my approach so that when I walked up to any group, within seconds they'd be won over and receptive to the magic.

From Tatou it was a natural progression to private parties. The Tatou clientele often threw exclusive parties, so I began to get hired to do magic at some pretty interesting venues. I started out charging two hundred dollars to walk around the party for two hours, doing whatever effects I felt like doing. The money was good but, more important, I was learning how to cope with doing magic in situations that were less than ideal. Invariably the room was noisy, the music was blaring, and I was trying to do effects for men whose attention would wander whenever a pretty woman would walk by.

It was an innocent time for me. I'd drive my beat-up old Honda to the parties and, more likely than not, stall en route, so I'd have to push the car to the side of the street and jump-start it. The Honda had no heater and no air conditioner, so on even the coldest nights I'd be forced to keep all the windows open so the windshield wouldn't fog up. I remember one night I finally convinced this girl that I'd been fantasizing about to go out on a date. It was one of the

Right, Left, Right, Left

This effect is reminiscent of the old game of someone hiding a coin or another small object in a hand and having the performer guess which hand contains the hidden object. What's great about it is that you do it to up to four people simultaneously, eliminating the possibility that it was a lucky guess.

You can do this effect with any coin. I prefer quarters. I line up three people in front of me, each one with a quarter. Then I turn my back to them and ask them to put the quarter in one of their hands and then hold that hand against their forehead and concentrate on it. I'd claim that I could get into a zone where I could pick up their vibrations and determine which hand the coin was in. But this will work only if they concentrate on sending me their thoughts, so I ask them to *really* concentrate and keep holding their hands to their foreheads.

I wait twenty to thirty seconds, then, right before I turn around, I tell them to lower both fists with their hands level and waist-high. Then I go down the line, pointing to one hand of each participant—"This one, this one, this one . . ."—until I choose a hand from each participant. When their hands are opened, I'm right every time.

Of course, I wasn't using any kind of thought transmission to guide me. I was just observing a simple principle of physiology. When you hold your hand up to your head for around thirty seconds, enough blood will drain out of it that when you bring it back down the hand that has been raised will be perceptibly lighter than the other hand. The veins in the raised hand will also be smoother. This works every time, and I won some nice side bets using this effect.

coldest nights of the year, and we drove to a movie theater in that old Honda. The outside of the windshield was frosted over, the windows were all down, she was huddled down in her seat shivering, and I was driving with my head sticking way out the window so I could see. Pretty embarrassing.

Then I got a job doing magic at a bar mitzvah party, and it changed my life. I met an owner of a big sporting goods company who offered me my then going rate, $1,500 for five hours' work at his son's affair. I didn't respond. I just told him to get a deck of cards

South Park *making fun of me*

and call me back the next day. I did This Is My Card over the phone, and it floored him. So I bumped my price up to $500 an hour, $2,500 for the night, which was a huge increase in pay.

At the bar mitzvah I was going from person to person doing magic when someone walked up to me and said, "Jeffrey Steiner would like to talk to you." He led me to an older man who gave me his business card. I was immediately impressed because he had phone numbers at all his different offices around the world. He was there with his beautiful wife, a Swedish woman named Irya. Jeffrey's a Turkish Jew with a strong accent. "Haf you ever been to Saint-Tropez?" he asked me. Saint-Tropez? I didn't know what it was *or* how to pronounce it. In fact, except for going to summer camp or visiting relatives in Florida, I'd hardly ever left the metropolitan New York area. "You have to come to my house there. It's a beautiful place in the South of France. I will have many guests, you'll do magic for them and make yourself some money," Jeffrey said.

After the party I did a little research on Mr. Steiner. It turned out he owned a company that was a very large contractor for NASA. He was totally legitimate, a solid family man—and a billionaire. So I was going to France. I told my mom about the Saint-Tropez trip, and she was thrilled for me. In the back of my mind, I felt bad about leaving her, even for just a week, since she was going through such an ordeal fighting off her cancer, but she insisted that she was fine and that I should go. I immediately went out and bought a funny little round hat and a small backpack for the rest of my clothes. I still had cash from the bar mitzvah party, so I treated my mother and my brother to lunch. It was a going-away party on two levels—I was traveling to Europe *and* I was quitting my job waiting tables. I had my bag with me because Jeffrey Steiner was sending a car to take me to the airport. Shortly after we finished eating, the car came and we left the restaurant. Out on the street, my mom seemed so proud of me; she just kept smiling and hugging me. It was a great feeling to be able to reward her a little bit for all the sacrifices she had made for me. Then it was time to go.

It was weird sitting in the back of a big black Lincoln Town Car for the first time. My perception had been that anyone who rode in one of those had big bucks. At the airport, I fell in at the back of a long line and waited for almost twenty minutes until it was my turn to check in. I handed my ticket to the counter representative and she smiled at me. "You didn't have to wait in this line. You're flying first

Ben Steiner (second from right) *and his entourage in Bodrum, Turkey*

class." I didn't even know the difference. All I knew was the round-trip ticket cost about $2,700. At that realization, it even occurred to me that I should just cash the ticket in, buy a cheaper seat, and keep the difference. It wasn't such a far-fetched idea. I didn't have much cash with me, and I certainly didn't have a credit card. If things didn't work out in Saint-Tropez, I wouldn't even have the option of calling a taxi and checking into a hotel. I was going to Europe for the first time in my life. Other than the Steiners, with whom I'd spent maybe a half hour, tops, I didn't know a soul there.

In France, a chauffeur who drove a fancy Mercedes picked me up. I sat back, and we took off down the coast. After a while we pulled into the grounds of the Steiners' home. The first thing I saw was a big pad for a helicopter. Then we passed two tennis courts, an Olympic-sized pool, a huge main house, and many smaller houses on one side of the property. I'd never dreamed that houses like this existed. The garage was loaded with every car you could imagine. There was a full discotheque in the basement of the main house, two yachts fully staffed at all times and featuring cuisine prepared by world-famous chefs. Walking around the main house was like being in a fine museum of contemporary art—original Picassos and Dalís hung on the walls. There was even a Warhol in the kitchen. I had been so excited to get there that I was the first person to arrive, so I was housed in one of the employee buildings. Even the maid's quarters had all the amenities of a Four Seasons hotel room.

After a few days the rest of the family, including Ben, Jeffrey's

sixteen-year-old son, came. I had met Ben at the bar mitzvah, and we immediately disliked each other. The first time I approached him, I asked if he wanted to see some magic, and he just blew me off, saying, "I already know it." I took him for a spoiled rich kid, and he probably pegged me as some low-life street hustler, but after spending a few days together, we became very close. Even though we came from opposite sides of the social spectrum, we found that we had a lot in common. And Ben took a great delight in introducing me to experiences that I had never even dreamed about. Every time I'd eat some new exotic food that was a revelation to me, Ben's face would light up. After a week I had moved into the main house, sharing a room with him (with two beds, of course).

Saint-Tropez

To say that Saint-Tropez was unlike anything I'd ever imagined would be an understatement. Being there was like finding yourself in the middle of a movie that was too over the top to believe. The most beautiful women, amazing cuisine, the most pristine beaches during the day, fantastic clubs after nightfall—the whole experience was beyond my wildest fantasies. Nobody in town really knew why I was there or who I was, but they knew that I was somehow connected to the Steiner family, so when we walked up to the huge lines that snaked outside of the exclusive clubs, the bouncers would part all the rich and famous people like the Red Sea, grabbing Ben and me and pulling us through the crowd. It was in one of those clubs where I met Jack Nicholson. I'd always been a big fan of his and had watched every one of his movies over and over again. At first, I almost didn't even want to approach him. I remember reading about Martin Scorsese's reaction when he found out he was at the same party as Akira Kurosawa, his favorite director. Scorsese turned around and walked right out the door, fearful that by seeing Kurosawa in the flesh, he'd discover that his idol had clay feet.

But this was too good an opportunity to pass up. I went over to Nicholson and did some card effects that astounded him. Soon we were sitting at the same table, talking about everything from women to our mutual admiration for the film *Wild at Heart.* Jack was friendly and charming, and it was a relief to see that behind that famous façade was a normal, cool guy. I was learning quickly. Up till then I

BURIED ALIVE

STRAPPED IN STRAIT JACKET

SECURED IN CASKET

BURIED UNDER SAND AND SECURELY LOCKED IN GIANT VAULT

HARRY HOUDINI'S ORIGINAL CREATION

"FREE!"

ESCAPING FROM A QUADRUPLE SMOTHERING IMPRISONMENT UNDER TONS OF SAND.

HOWARD ELCOCK

HOUDINI

PRESENTS
HIS OWN ORIGINAL INVENTION
THE GREATEST SENSATIONAL MYSTERY
EVER ATTEMPTED IN THIS OR ANY OTHER AGE

$1,000 REWARD TO ANY ONE PROVING THAT IT IS POSSIBLE TO OBTAIN AIR IN THE "UP-SIDE-DOWN" POSITION IN WHICH HOUDINI RELEASES HIMSELF FROM THIS WATER FILLED TORTURE CELL

HARRY HOUDINI

KING OF CARDS

NATIONAL PTG. & ENG. CO. CHICAGO

(left) *Houdini created this amazing poster to advertise a live onstage buried-alive feat. He never performed it.*
(top) *Houdini's Water Torture Cell;*
(above) *An early poster from before his escape-artist days*

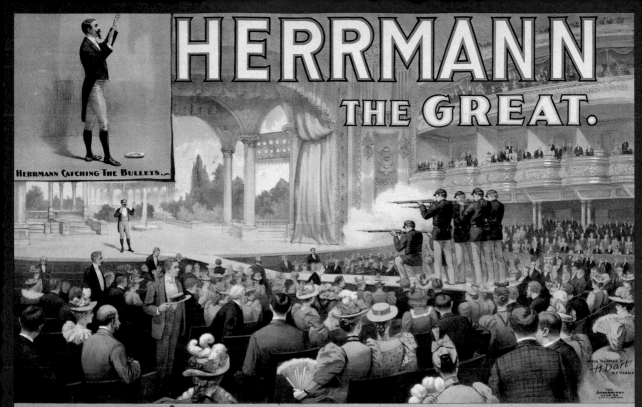

HERRMANN
THE GREAT.

HERRMANN CATCHING THE BULLETS.

HERRMANN'S MARVELOUS BULLET CATCHING FEAT
PERFORMED AT THE METROPOLITAN OPERA HOUSE IN AID OF THE NEW YORK HERALD FREE ICE FUND.

Herrmann The Great

KELLAR

(above) *Herrmann performed his bullet catch only a few times, always to a large audience and huge publicity.*
(left) *The great American magician Harry Kellar*

(top) *George de la Tour's painting of card cheats;* (bottom left) *Chung Ling Soo was an American named Billy Robinson, who started out as an assistant to Herrmann. He became famous in England performing as a Chinese magician.*
(bottom right) *A fourteenth-century representation of a pillar saint.*

(left top and bottom) *Two cards from the very old and beautiful Visconti-Sforza Tarot deck;* (right) *Dali's* Christ of St. John of the Cross

Tarquo the Great (1939–2001), one of the great close-up magicians

had the idea that rich people were somehow different, a class unto themselves that you had to be born into. But as I met more and more people in Saint-Tropez, I realized that a lot of them were self-made millionaires (and billionaires), so that whole mystique that surrounded the rich and famous began to dissolve. I realized that one could sit down one-on-one with just about anybody and have a really interesting conversation. Every night I'd accompany the Steiners to ridiculously elaborate dinner parties, and by then I wasn't intimidated by anybody, so all of a sudden, I became this enigmatic character. It was quite a role-reversal for a young kid who grew up in Brooklyn and was on his own for the first time in his life. Instead of staying for a week, as I'd originally intended, I ended up staying three months. During that time, my whole world expanded exponentially. We took trips to Italy and Germany. One morning Jeffrey woke us and told us we were going to his house in Turkey. So we piled into his private plane and flew to Istanbul.

When the summer finally ended, I came back to New York, but everything had changed. I had a whole new perspective on life. For one thing, I decided that I wouldn't do restaurant magic anymore. Even before I left for Saint-Tropez, I had realized that I couldn't get to the next level by going from table to table in restaurants doing magic. You just can't have big dreams and not go for them. Besides, I had been transformed by my experiences overseas. I had a new-found confidence that I could actually make a conscious effort and will my own success. In France, right before I returned, I'd woken up one morning, stared into the mirror, and begun to shave off all my

Performing magic for the president

hair. At the same time, I had been growing a goatee, and this new look seemed to be a tangible manifestation of my inner transformation.

I returned to New York, and, as luck would have it, the dad of a friend of mine from acting school was a big magic aficionado who also owned several apartments in the superexclusive Sherry-Netherland Hotel. One tiny apartment of his was empty, so he let me stay there for the same rent I had been paying to crash on my friend's couch. Of course this exclusive address fed into my newly acquired high-maintenance lifestyle. I began to wander around Manhattan, dropping into the hottest, trendiest clubs. I'd perform some magic, blow everyone away, and then leave. I wasn't networking; I didn't hang on the people that I had mystified and try to get their business cards. It was the opposite of networking—I'd bestow some amazement on people and ask for and expect nothing in return. Of course, human nature what it is, when one doesn't appear needy, people will go out of their way trying to help; unfortunately the converse is often also true.

But all these considerations paled in light of the most serious problem I faced when I returned. While I was in Europe, my mom had veered off the macrobiotic regimen, and her cancer had roared back tri-fold. She didn't want to tell me about her relapse while I was away because she was afraid of ruining my summer, but by now her disease had advanced at a horrific rate. I'll never forget the feeling of finding out the horrible news. It was like walking into a room blindfolded and getting smacked in the face with a baseball bat. My

I pulled my heart out of my chest on **Last Call with Carson Daly.**
NBC threatened not to air it.

mom was bedridden, and she'd lost a large amount of weight. I was anxious to tell her about all the good things that had happened to me, but it was hard for her to comprehend because the doctors were giving her tremendous doses of morphine for her pain. Even then she never complained, just like she never complained when she first started fighting her cancer and I had to help her walk up four flights of stairs to her job teaching underprivileged kids, because her legs had swollen to four times their normal size due to the radiation treatments.

I spent the last few weeks of her life in bed with her. It was hard for me to fathom that she was dying. I had always envisioned succeeding at magic so I could shower my mom with all the material things she had sacrificed in order to give me every advantage as a child. But she was never one for material things. She lived a truly spiritual life—never judging, always trusting, always loving. By the end she could hardly even speak, but I'll never forget her last words. She looked at me and said, "God is love." Even though she was too weak to talk, she kept clinging to life. It wasn't until a few days later when I read through her journals that I found out why. She had written that her big worry was that after she was gone, I'd be all alone in the world. She was holding on and struggling because she was afraid of that prospect.

I got back into bed with her and held her. I told her that she had given me everything that I needed to prepare me for going out in the world and achieving my goals. I assured her that I had people I loved. "It's okay, Ma, you can stop fighting. I'm going to be okay," I whispered. It's the hardest thing in the world to tell that to the person you love more than anything. She didn't respond. About half an hour later, I felt a huge surge of energy that seemed to resonate right through my body, and I felt the release and knew that my mom had moved on. She had always said that she didn't want people to react to her death by crying, since dying was just a part of life, and that after she was gone, we should celebrate her life and be joyous, not sad. I desperately wanted to feel that with every fiber of my being, but even though I knew she had gone on to a better place, the pain was too intense, and I heard the deepest, most gut-wrenching sound a human can produce come out of my mouth.

"I saw the angel in the marble and carved until I set him free"
—Michelangelo, referring to his statue of David.

CHAPTER VII
THE MAN AIN'T RIGHT

*Sooner or later in life
everyone discovers that perfect
happiness is unrealizable, but
there are few who pause to
consider the antithesis: that
perfect unhappiness is equally
unattainable.*

–Primo Levi, *Survival in Auschwitz*

The Man Ain't Right

I was completely alone. Stranded. The one constant in my life was gone, and without her everything was spinning out of control. The only thing that would lift my spirits was magic, so I became obsessed. I'd read, study, practice—I put everything I had into the art. With my mom gone, I had nothing more to lose, and when you have nothing to lose, you have everything to gain. I had no fear. And I had no home. I couldn't stand living at the Sherry-Netherland anymore. I went back to crashing on a friend's couch, ironically in the same building in Little Italy where I had stayed with my actor friend. After five months of living in a fantasy world, I had come full circle.

Then I started dreaming again. I fantasized about creating something new in magic—a magician whose stage was the real world, who could touch people of any race, any religion, any age, any ethnicity. I started visiting jails and hospitals and old-age homes and performed magic behind those institutional walls. What I saw just reinforced my belief that all people are the same. It's a universal defense mechanism for people to build walls around themselves to survive. The older you are, the more layers you've built. Magic shatters those barriers. Michelangelo was once asked how he could create such beautiful sculptures out of cold slabs of marble, and he said, "I saw the angel in the marble and carved until I set him free." That's what magic does. Magic allows people to recapture their childlike wonder and strip away their defenses. Magic makes people vulnerable. That's when they're the most beautiful, because they're no longer hiding and no longer afraid.

We live in an electronic age, in a global village, as Marshall McLuhan noted, so I instinctively knew that I'd have to do my magic on television. The only problem was that growing up I had never watched TV. My mother never allowed a television in our house; she would rather have seen me reading a book or learning by interacting with real people. It wasn't until I started visiting the

"Okay, hold the box . . . Just think of your card.

Keep thinking. Keep thinking . . . Look, one card."

"I'm really shaking." [whimpering] "I'm going into labor" "Take the card out. Is this your card?

"Yes . . . I can't believe this man."

Museum of Broadcasting and watching vintage tapes of magicians that I saw the way magic had been previously presented on TV. None of it made any sense to me. When I did my magic to people, the important thing was their reaction and the communication between us. That dynamic was never depicted on the televised magic shows I saw. I couldn't understand why no magician had focused on the reactions of the people he was doing magic to. I knew that's what I would do.

My first step was to shoot a demo tape. I persuaded a friend who had a video camera to go out on the street with me one afternoon and film me doing magic to people who weren't ready for it. We hadn't walked more than a few blocks from my apartment in Little Italy when I approached three people. They had their guard up when I did the first card effect, but by the second one they'd started screaming and jumping up and down. One of the guys was so astounded he actually ran right into traffic and narrowly avoided getting hit by a car. Right then I knew we had a show.

At the end of the day, I went back to the apartment, borrowed a friend's VCR, plugged it into my other friend's VCR, did a quick edit, and ended up with fifteen minutes of really strong footage. Now I had a demo tape. The next step was to get an agent. Through a friend I met a music agent at ICM named Jonny Podell. He loved my demo but was skeptical that this type of magic would work for an entire show. But with one foot in the door at ICM, I was relentless. I'd hang around the offices and do magic for all the other agents. They all had the same reaction: Great stuff but will it play on TV?

Meanwhile, I kept honing my skills. Around that time, I started meeting a lot of up-and-coming artists, actors, and directors. We were all young, all talking about our big plans and how we were going to change our respective industries. Everywhere I went I viewed as a place to advance my magic. Being in New York meant that my path crossed those of a lot of people who were respected in their fields. It was a thrill to be mystifying people who I'd watched and studied when I was growing up. I did magic for everyone all the time—Madonna, Michael Jordan, Al Pacino, Mike Tyson, Robert De Niro, Spike Lee. And their reactions were so strong that accounts

I was lucky to find these three amazing girls for my first TV show.

of my magic began showing up in the local papers. A buzz began.

Around the same time, MTV began airing funny interstitial spots between videos. I thought these would be the perfect place for me to do short pieces of magic, so I targeted MTV's Broadway offices. I began by walking up to the hall secretary on the main floor and doing magic to her. She introduced me to a producer who brought me in to do magic for his staff.

They were all amazed and kept introducing me to their bosses, and eventually I had a meeting with the president of programming. I did some magic, pitched him my idea, and he said, "Great. Done." I was offered a five-year deal. The only problem was that it was an exclusive contract, which meant I couldn't do magic anywhere else. Even though I was still crashing on a couch, I instinctively knew that if I did that deal I might be so overplayed that after five years I'd end up with nothing. So I turned it down.

The fact that I even got an offer from MTV made my agents at ICM see me in a new light. One day I was hanging out at their offices when Stu Bloomberg, a vice president at ABC, happened to drop by. I did magic for him, and he reacted strongly. Next thing I knew my agent had a meeting set up with the president of ABC. This was it.

The night before the meeting, I scribbled all my ideas on a piece of paper. I proposed to do a program that would show real magic in real places, immediate and honest. We'd go all over the country and

Staten Island Sunday Advance

TVmag

APRIL 11, 1999

The man who fell to Earth

Magician and escape artist David Blaine is featured in a new special, "Street Magic," airing Wednesday night at 10

See story, Page TV 3

show the reactions of people of all races, religions, creeds, and classes to my magic, basically exposing the beautiful side of humanity—capturing those pure moments of awe, the innocent moments when people drop their masks and stop critiquing themselves or obsessing on their everyday problems.

I walked into the office of Ted Harbert, who was then the president of ABC, with this little, crinkled-up piece of paper. And my magic. I started off by asking him to think of a card. He did. I riffled through the deck, but I couldn't find it in there. Then I pointed to his window. The glass was sealed off, there was no way you could open the window, but there, on the other side of the glass, was his card. Then I had Ted take out his own deck of cards, and his secretary and I went to an adjoining conference room and did a really strong card effect over the speakerphone. When I nailed the card, all the ABC executives went crazy, and my agent started screaming, "I quit. I'm not working for the devil anymore." They were ready to offer a deal, but I was taking no chances.

While they were still recovering from the over-the-phone card effect, I told them that I wanted to show them one last crazy thing I really liked. I started walking around the room, feeling the furniture, knocking on the floor, tapping on the walls, until I found a spot in front of a big window. Then I just stood there, closed my eyes, and levitated. They all screamed and ran out of their own office. When they finally calmed down, they said, "What do we have to do to keep you from going somewhere else?" My agent told them we wanted a million dollars and a guarantee for a large number of prime-time commercials. (Eventually, Spike Lee directed them.) I also wanted to own all the footage and all the rights to it. The next day they came back to us with a yes to everything. There I was, living on a couch, with a check in my pocket for $375,000, my first installment.

I knew that you get only one chance, so I put everything I had into my shot. The first thing I did was find a producer. I didn't know all that much about TV, but I knew I had a strong idea—a reality-TV magic show—that had never been done before. I was hanging

The Dallas Cowboys

out with my friend the great filmmaker Harmony Korine, and he told me I had to see this new show called *COPS*. We watched it, and I was blown away. It was poignant and intriguing and edgy, all at the same time. I researched who was responsible for putting that show on Fox, and I found my producer, a guy named Steven Chao.

The more I learned about Chao the more I liked him. He was a kid who came from nothing and went to Harvard, then worked his way up to running a network. While he was at Fox, he did a corporate presentation about free speech and hired a male stripper to get up onstage and do a striptease in the middle of his presentation. The wife of one of the Fox executives was so upset by the stripper that Chao was ordered to get him off the stage. Since the whole point was free speech, Chao refused and made the guy dance longer. He was fired soon afterward.

Now the story gets even more interesting. When he was fired Chao got a multimillion-dollar payout. He was living in a nice house with a live-in maid, but he wanted to remember what working-class people have to face every day. So he stashed his uncashed check in his desk and went and got a job at McDonald's. Every day he would surreptitiously dress in his McDonald's uniform and sneak out of the house so his maid didn't see him going to work. I liked that.

I had a good idea what effects I wanted to do on the show, but I still needed to do some work on the character I was creating, so I got in touch with an amazing magician named Paul Harris. He had already changed my life. I was ten years old when my mother brought home one of Paul's books. *A Close-Up Kind of Guy* enthralled me with

With Paul Harris, one of my early mentors

The magic isn't in the trick, it's in the eyes.

all these incredibly inventive card effects. When I finally met Paul years later, we became instant friends.

There's an intense mystical aura around Paul. I think part of it stems from the time his house burned to the ground. Everything he owned—his books, his magic, his possessions—went up in smoke. Whereas some people would run out and get insurance and try to buy back all their stuff, Paul did something different. He wanted to explore what was behind the magic, and he went for it.

Paul became a nomad, hitting the road with only the clothes on his back. To this day, he wanders from town to town like some mendicant priest miraculously making his way. If he runs out of money, the phone suddenly rings, and it's a publishing company trying to track him down to send him back-royalties from one of his old books. Almost every effect that Paul produces now has some charitable quality to it. He's living magic.

Paul suggested that we rent a little cabin outside Estes Park, Colorado, and brainstorm. We spent an amazing week together. Crazy things happen when you're in Paul's presence. Normally skittish deer came right up to him and ate food out of his hand. Later we were wandering around Estes Park, looking for a place to eat, engrossed in a conversation about Jesus, and right when we turned a corner and opened the door to go into a restaurant, we bumped into someone on his way out. "Jesus!" he said. I looked at Paul. "You guys scared me," the guy said, and walked away.

One night we were in some quiet bar watching a few locals play darts. They weren't very good, but all of a sudden Paul yelled out, "Bull's-eye!" and the guy threw his dart, bam, right into the bull's-eye. That night some girls came up to us, and I told one girl her name, her mother's name, her birthday. Everything was just "on." Paul was walking around the whole time going "Ommm. Ommm. Ommm." I just knew everything we were formulating was exactly right.

After a week we had fashioned a unique, consistent character for the show—sort of an urban shaman, an unexplainable, mysterious, but ultimately real guy who walks up to people in the street, is in their lives for a moment, then out of their lives, after having added some amazement to their day.

Now I had a character, and I also had a name for the show—*Street Magic*. Ironically enough, I had never done street magic before, but I always thought that it was better to have a title that underplayed the show. Most other magic shows on TV had grandiose titles like *The World's Greatest Magic Show;* when you tried to get through them, though, they were unwatchable. I figured it was better to underplay the name and hope that it would be a better magic program than anybody had previously seen.

Besides Paul Harris, I enlisted Michael Weber, another magician friend of mine, to help me out. Weber's a brilliant mentalist-hypnotist, but he also does incredible magic. I've seen him just nail people many times. One night I was with him in a club; we were talking about hypnotism, and I asked him for a demonstration. Weber looked around the room and spotted a big, scary-looking Russian guy who was there with his friend and their two young wives. He told me he was going to give the big guy's wife a posthypnotic suggestion that would make her break down in tears when she heard a certain phrase. I could even choose the phrase. Just to mess with him, I chose "clown suit," a phrase that I was sure would make her laugh.

Weber walked right up to the guy's wife, pulled her aside, and within a minute had her passed out and lying on the couch while he whispered in her ear, right in front of her brute of a husband. Then he snapped his fingers, and *boom,* she woke right up. The four of us started a normal conversation; then Weber gave me the nod. I had been saying some humorous things, and everyone was in a great mood when I said, "It looks like that guy's wearing a clown suit." As soon as the words were out of my mouth, this girl went into hysterics. She was gushing tears, and her husband started to look concerned, so Weber just said, "And you're out," and he snapped his fingers, and the girl went from crying to being fast asleep, just like that. Then he whispered some words into her ear, snapped his fingers, and she was smiling again. She remembered nothing; she was just curious about why her face was a little wet. That's Weber.

This is a Paul Harris effect that can be done in someone's house or at a coffee shop or anywhere there's a supply of sugar packets. You write down a prediction of a number from one to six. Fold it up and put it to the side. Then take a pen and consecutively number the first six sugar packets. Tell your friends that the side with the number on it is considered heads, the blank side tails. Have one of them take the six packets into her hand, shake them a little to shuffle them, then throw them onto the table. The ones that land heads up

"I just came from the welfare department. I have nothing; he offered me nothing, just said he wanted to show me something. I'm fifty years old and what he showed to me is mind-boggling. I don't care if he makes a million or starves to death, it doesn't make a difference, it's mind-boggling. Whatever the hell it is."

Card through window

(numbered) she keeps, the blank ones she discards. She keeps doing this until she's left with one numbered packet. Then you unfold your prediction. It's the correct number.

The way you can predict this 100 percent of the time takes a bit of preparation. Before everyone is congregated, you write one number on one of the first six packets. You might count down to the fourth packet and write a "4" on one side. Later, when everyone's at the table, you offer to show them something. Take out your pen and start marking the numbers on the first six sugar packets. The fourth one, which you've previously secretly marked, now has the number "4" on both sides of it, so when you flip the packets, it will never come blank-side up. Inevitably, the "4" packet will win, just as you predicted.

We had a great time filming *Street Magic*. We were just a bunch of young, hungry people, touring the country in a beat-up bus, living out of Motel 6's. We didn't have a fifty-person crew with people sitting around eating doughnuts; everybody was doing everything. A lot of times during filming the crowd would get so big that when we stopped shooting, people would walk off before they had signed releases. I'd be running down the block after them going, "I need your release."

Hanging out with a bunch of magicians is unlike anything you

could ever imagine. They all have a crazy sense of humor, and most of them have these huge egos, so they're always trying to bust each other up. Plus, they're just strange. Take Weber. He's a really serious-looking guy who gets big bucks to demonstrate mentalism at corporate conventions, yet he's the biggest kid in the world. He walks around with gadgets that you wouldn't believe a grown man would have.

One day Weber got his hands on some light-emitting diodes and put them into his mouth, so when he talked to you each tooth would light up with a different color. We'd be ready to start shooting, and I'd look for Weber and find him sitting on the grass, making a pen float out of a bottle. Of course, I didn't exactly act like an executive either. Since we both had pretty large egos, Steve Chao and I would get into some pretty heated arguments, which we'd resolve by wrestling each other right in the middle of the street. We were playing around, but it was definitely rough playing around.

There were so many ups and downs during the shoot. The lowest was in Atlantic City. I had been doing magic to this group of girls, and they gave me the best reactions I'd ever gotten. I was totally psyched, but then, right when we were done, I looked at the camera and noticed that the RECORD light was off. None of the footage was there. I walked straight into a casino, pulled a couple of grand out of my pocket, and just blew it. I lost the money, I lost the footage, I was sure that the show was going to hell. I was so miserable I almost couldn't shoot for the next two days.

We wound up shooting in New York, Dallas, San Francisco, and the Mojave Desert, but my favorite segment was shot in Compton, California. We were scouting a location in an anonymous-looking tinted-window van. After a while we spotted a corner where some guys were just hanging out, so I had the driver pull over. I jumped out of the van and turned to the crew, but every one of them was too frightened to get out, so I figured I'd go out alone and do some magic so the brothers would warm up to me; then we'd get the crew in. The only problem was I forgot that I was wearing a mike wired to my shirt, so when I walked up to the guys on the corner, they took one look, pegged me as a fed, and started running away.

I had to chase one guy halfway down the block and bowl him over with some magic before all the others came back. By then my crew was finally bold enough to get out of the van and start filming.

People attach a stigma to others based on where they live or what they look like, but these Compton guys were really nice. We ended up shooting there for two hours, and when we left my whole crew and the Compton guys were high-fiving and hugging one another.

I put everything I had into the show. I even got my friend Leonardo Di Caprio to do the narration. I was so intent on shooting more than enough good material that we were running out of money. Now it was time to edit it all down. I had previously seen a great documentary called *Crumb,* so I hired the guy who edited that to work on my show. Every day Steve Chao and I would spend hour after hour in that editing room. It was a lot of work but a great education.

I was drained but happy when we finished the final edit. The show had card effects, some coin work, some mentalism, and we ended it with a few different levitations. All done on the street, for free, right in the faces of people who just happened to have a chance encounter with a mysterious stranger. Young black kids, old Chinese guys, Jewish women on an excursion to Atlantic City, tattooed, pierced people in the East Village and the Haight-Ashbury—we really did prove that magic is universal, the great equalizer. We even shot me doing effects to some of the Dallas Cowboys, which added a whole other level to the show, because now we had the world's most serious hard-core football team running around screaming like kids. Everyone knew that no one could pay these football players enough to act like that, and their reactions were so good they validated the reactions of the rest of the people in the show.

The segment with the Cowboys proved that my instincts were right—what made this show so innovative was focusing on the reactions of the people who had just had magic done to them. Shock,

Shooting in Compton, California

laughter, astonishment, awe, incredulity, stunned silence—it was an amazing range. But the levitation floored everyone. We hadn't originally planned on using the levitation to end the show, but it turned out better than we could have dreamed.

We got such great reviews that my eyes teared up when I read them, wishing my mom was around to be part of all this. Unfortunately, the show wasn't promoted too well, so the ratings for the first half weren't that great. We picked up a couple million viewers by the second half, though, so I guess whoever stumbled onto the special must have called their friends and told them to tune in. Even though the network wasn't thrilled that the show wasn't a huge ratings success, I didn't really care. *Street Magic* was everything I'd dreamed of for years and more. Step one had been accomplished.

W.W. TOTER

CHAPTER VIII

PRIMITIVE MYSTERIES

Primitive Mysteries

was staring intently at a woman. I'd just said to her, "Think of someone in your life who's important to you." Her whole demeanor changed; she started to look a little nervous. This was the final day of shooting my second special, *Magic Man,* and we were losing light fast—this would be the last possible shot and we had to get it.

"The name is short," I said. She made eye contact. Her body language made me think I might be right. I also sensed that it was a woman's name, probably someone close to her. "And the name symbolizes something else," I said. Her eyes widened. I knew in my gut, just by intuition, that I was right. At that exact moment a truck drove by with WHITE ROSE, the name of the company, printed on the side. She didn't see the truck because her back was to it. I thought that the appearance of the word "Rose" at that precise moment was too fortunate to be simply a coincidence, and my hunch was that it was the name she was thinking of, so I turned her around so she could see the truck. At that same moment, a cab drove by with the word DAWN spray-painted in huge letters on its side. She saw it, started screaming, and then broke down crying. I didn't even see DAWN on the cab (in fact, we had to find the cab on the film later; even our cameraman hadn't seen it), but when she reacted so strongly, that was the name that immediately came to mind. I intuitively understood from the depth of her emotion that Dawn was her mother and that she had passed away. Some might say this was that strange place where coincidence plays into reality, but when it hits on this level, it seems to be more than a coincidence, as if there's some other force at work. We got our last, crucial shot.

My modus operandi when we're doing these street shoots is simple. I just approach people who look interesting or bizarre or eccentric—the kinds of people that I'm normally attracted to. We have a goal with the magic in mind, but it's always spontaneous and random, never predictable. Most of the time people will respond favorably, I'll do an effect, and we'll have some footage. Sometimes

"There's a spark of magic in your eyes."

people run away. Either way, it's never set up in advance. What you see is what we got.

We shot one of my favorite segments for *Magic Man* on the first day of shooting in New York. Again, it was near the end of the day; we were losing light when we came upon a homeless guy sitting in front of the gates of an ornate old church on lower Fifth Avenue. It was cool out, and he had a wool blanket pulled over his legs. I rushed over to him, and the camera crew followed, not knowing what was going to happen. The guy had a cup of take-out coffee with the lid still on it. I leaned over and grabbed the cup. "Let me show you something," I said. "Take the lid off the coffee and taste it, make sure it's not too hot." He complied. "Watch," I said, and I began to swirl the cup slowly, holding it in both my hands. I muttered some weird incantations, and the coffee in the cup turned into coins.

"How'd you do that?" the homeless guy said. "Oh, that's pure magic."

"This is for you," I said, and handed him the cup full of change.

"Oh, you son of a gun," he said, tears welling up in his eyes. "Thank you, guys, this is the best yet." Then he broke into an impromptu song—"There's a spark of magic in your eyes"—and reached up and hugged me. We ultimately closed the show with this guy.

The story doesn't end there. After we finished shooting, I wound up giving this guy the rest of the money I had in my pocket— a couple of hundred dollars. Coincidentally, the night I started working on this chapter, recounting this story, I took a break, went outside to get something, and ran into the same homeless guy outside the church. It was freezing that night, so I invited him up to my apartment and ordered some ice cream from the corner deli. He wolfed it down, I made him a bubble bath, and he was so happy. He stayed with me overnight, had a good night's sleep, a hearty breakfast, got some new clothes, and then went on his way.

After the New York shoot, we took to the road. Most of *Magic Man* was scheduled to be shot in cities I hadn't used in my first special. I was excited because on this show I was getting a chance to work with one of my closest friends, Bill Kalush.

I'll never forget the first time I met Kalush. It was at Reuben's, a midtown delicatessen that was a meeting place for New York area magicians. Kalush walked into the deli with Michael Weber, pulled out a deck of cards, and did this thing called Ascension, in which a face-up card mysteriously rises by itself through the deck, like a hot knife going through butter, until it floats right to the top. It was one of the most amazing moves I'd ever seen—every one of the forty magicians there was blown away. Seconds later Kalush turned around and walked out. The rest of the day that was all anybody talked about.

I'd see Kalush from time to time at Reuben's, and mostly we talked about movies. We had similar sensibilities, so we connected on that level. I had previously seen him do a card move called the Simple Switch, so one day I cornered him and asked him to show it to me again. Kalush took out a deck of cards and divided it into two piles, one for each hand, cards face up. Then he flipped the top card on each pile over to the other pile. It was like a juggling act with

King Richard chills in the tub.

A READING

We went to extraordinary lengths for this book. We actually convinced the publisher to print a number of variations, knowing that greatly diverse people would be reading it. It's not chance that you're reading this particular version.

You may know me, but I know you.

You're a very sensitive type of person.

When you were younger, you were different from the others around you. You were observant. You'd silently take in a situation and notice things about the people in your presence. Your intuition is strong.

You are very caring and honest, sometimes even too much so, but you have great difficulty in letting anybody get to know you. When you finally do let somebody in, you keep him or her close to you for a long time. In fact, there's someone close to you that you're really worried about right now. But the best thing to do is to keep being a positive force in that person's life.

Sometimes you're overly analytic, but it's better to try to live spontaneously.

You have a scar on your left knee.

Now before you begin to think that I'm psychic and can look into the depths of your soul, and do it through this book, let me explain how I was just able to tell you so much about yourself. What I did is an example of something called cold reading, an old technique used by psychics to make their subjects believe in the psychics' intuition and convince them that the psychics can predict their futures.

It's called "cold" reading because at first the reader knows little or nothing about the person being read. But by simple deduction from the client's body language, posture, breathing rate, eye contact, and other non-verbal cues, the cold reader is able to assess what general category the person being read falls into, and then he or she begins a well-planned formulaic reading for that type. Cold reading is a finely honed system of generalizations that are employed to make it appear as if the reader has powers that enable him to penetrate into the life of the person being read. By the way, most people have scars on their left knees.

Since cold reading is an art of generalization, it's important for the reader to know up-to-the-minute demographic facts about different classes

of people, but it's also important to have the facility to read people and see how they react as you expound about them. Very often when you say a generality, the person who's being read will agree and then reveal even more about herself than you mentioned. Just be sensitive and pick up on it. The more you develop this gift, the more you can take shots in the dark and nail them.

In the 1980s and 1990s, an amazing psychic named Herb Dewey wrote a series of books aimed at an audience of fellow psychics, although many mentalists in the magic field bought them. They were filled with practical tips for doing cold readings that Dewey had amassed during his long career, which included over 100,000 personal readings. Dewey's techniques were genius. He would start a cold reading by asking his client, "How long are you here for?" If his client was visiting from out of town, he or she was immediately impressed and predisposed to read into anything he would say from that point on. But if the client was from that same area and questioned what Dewey meant, he'd just say, "I meant how long is the reading you want, a half hour or a full hour?" Either way, he didn't lose.

The best of Dewey's books is called *King of the Cold Readers,* and it includes a phrase to remind his pupils to cover all the seven basic categories that people who come for readings want addressed. The phrase was THE SCAM, and it came from the first letter of each category word: travel, health, expectations, sex, career, ambitions, and money. The odds are that one of those categories is the one the person being read is most concerned with.

For example, Dewey told his readers that, when you talk about travel, you should cover your bases and mention both a long and a short trip. Then he had the readers add, "With respect to travel, you appear to have the desire to return to the past. I am not exactly sure what that means, but I sense a desire to return to the past." Everybody can obviously read into that statement.

When it came to health, Dewey cautioned against giving medical advice but told the readers to routinely tell their clients that they can see them living into their eighties or nineties. Who can argue with that kind of prediction? The rest of the categories are dealt with in the same generalized fashion.

→

Cold readers pick up on all available cues and incorporate them into their readings. For example, one cold reader felt that it was a godsend when a client paid him by check. By just looking at the check, the cold reader could tell when the account was opened, if the address on the check matched the address where the person was residing now, if insignias were present that would reveal hints about occupations or hobbies. A telephone number would allow him to call the person under a different pretext and get more information. An oversized check might indicate a business venture. A social security number on the check would allow the reader to determine where that person applied for his or her social security number (the first three numbers indicate that).

King of the Cold Readers is full of little deductive tips that would enable cold readers to nail their clients. If the psychic was reading a tall, lanky woman, Dewey advised the reader to say, "When you were growing up, and even now, to a lesser degree, you hated your feet." Most tall women feel self-conscious about the size of their feet. If the psychic was reading a person with dark shadows under her eyes, she was advised to look right at the person and say, "I see there's a problem or situation that bothers you, worries you, and keeps you awake at night." Of course, all women like to think they're psychic themselves, so Dewey suggested that readers look into their clients' eyes and say, "Your eyes are very magical, very mystical, very psychic."

Usually people don't want to hear anything negative when they're paying to learn about their future. That's why psychics generally agree that the most important thing is to leave the subject with hope. "You'll never get rich in this business peddling gloom," one psychic counseled.

cards, but it was impossible to do. "Don't even bother trying to learn it," he told me. "I've been doing it for ten years and I'm still working on it."

That was all I needed to hear. I spent the next three weeks practicing the Simple Switch for almost eight hours a day. Then I saw Kalush at one of the Park Avenue restaurants where I was doing my magic. "Hey, Bill, check this out," I said, and I took out a deck of cards and nailed the move. Kalush grabbed the cards and examined them, convinced that I was somehow cheating. We started to become great friends from that point on.

One of my favorite pieces of magic

Kalush is a magic purist. For him, magic is a serious pursuit. He never performs in public, but he's a scholar of magic history, with an amazing collection of magic books that date from the mid-1500s to the present. He's got a great conceptual mind. I was excited that I was going to be doing magic in some pretty primitive locations for this special. After we finished the rest of our U.S. shoots, we would go to a place where magic was so embedded in the culture that my levitation effect was greeted with yawns. It was no big deal to them that I floated six inches off the ground—everybody there was used to seeing their relatives change into cows. We were going to Haiti.

Many of the greatest magicians in history spent years touring the world. Houdini won his first acclaim in Europe and England. Kellar, the Herrmanns, Thurston, Dante all mounted elaborate world tours. Most of the time these tours went off without a hitch, but performing magic in a different culture sometimes presents great challenges and even perils. You've already read about Robert-Houdin's triumphant performances in Algeria in 1856. Thirty-five years later, the Foreign Office of Great Britain sent Douglas Beaufort, a British society magician, on a similar mission, this time to Fez, Morocco, to defuse the Marabout magic. Beaufort's magic was a huge success, or so he thought. Throughout his show the sultan of Morocco looked amazed and kept murmuring, *"Allah imtahal al Shitan!"* Later Beaufort had the sultan's pronouncement translated.

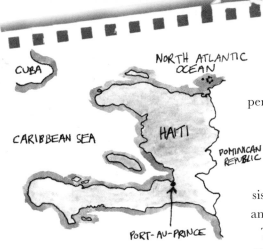

CUBA

NORTH ATLANTIC OCEAN

CARIBBEAN SEA

HAITI

DOMINICAN REPUBLIC

PORT-AU-PRINCE

He'd been saying, "God burn the devil!"

When cultures clash, the results can sometimes be perilous. Around the turn of the century the American magician Carl Hertz toured Borneo and performed for the raja. His presentation went over so well that the raja's daughter decided Hertz would marry her. When the magician declined and introduced her to his wife, she insisted and said that she would treat Hertz's wife as an equal and a sister—polygamy being the norm in Bornean society. The raja would be very, very upset if Hertz rejected her proposal, she added ominously.

Hertz thought quickly. He proposed a special show to celebrate the impending royal nuptials. That night he performed his famous Phoenix cremation, an illusion in which his wife was burned alive and then restored. But this time it was Hertz himself who was cremated. Unfortunately, the restoration part of the performance failed, and the real Mrs. Hertz cried hysterically over the "ashes." Meanwhile, behind the curtain, the magician was spirited off the raja's grounds and onto his ship in a basket used to store props. It was said that the raja's daughter was grief-stricken by her prospective husband's "passing."

Hertz got off easy compared with Andrew Oehler, a magician who performed at the beginning of the nineteenth century. Oehler was making a fortune staging balloon exhibitions and fireworks displays in Mexico. To show his appreciation, he mounted a special show for the governor of Mexico. He outfitted an old house with skeletons and sound effects and conducted a realistic séance for his audience of high-ranking officials. Candles snuffed out and relit themselves, ghosts materialized and spoke, lights blazed as thunder crashed and lightning flashed.

The next morning Oehler was arrested and thrown into an underground dungeon on charges of sorcery. Months later a member of Spanish royalty visited the Mexican governor and explained that Oehler's show had been done by perfectly natural scientific methods. The by now bearded magician was immediately released. When he returned to his lodging, he found that the innkeeper had disappeared with his equipment, clothes, and all of his considerable cash on hand. The repentant governor then offered Oehler a thousand dollars and two thousand acres of land if Oehler would become a Mexican citizen. Oehler took the money and left for New Orleans.

In his memoirs he wrote that he was convinced the real reason he was imprisoned was that the very religious Mexican officials were offended when he turned water into wine.

I didn't think I'd wind up in jail, but I didn't really know what to expect when we flew to Haiti. The first thing that hits you when you arrive is the unrelenting poverty. An average place in Haiti makes the favelas in Rio look like Club Med. Port-au-Prince, Haiti's largest city, has few amenities. There are few restaurants. Except for an occasional gas station, there are no stores. Everything is rubble. People live ten to a room in brick shanties on the mountainsides that continually get washed away when the big rainstorms come. We hooked up with Abujo, a well-connected guide who had hired a force of off-duty policemen to act as our bodyguards. We needed them, especially since we were carrying around a large amount of camera equipment.

On our first night in Haiti, Abujo had arranged for us to film a voodoo ceremony in the poorest part of Port-au-Prince, a neighborhood called Cité Soleil. We followed our police escort as they led us through a labyrinth of corridors between two large African-style buildings, but what was totally unnerving was that it was eleven o'clock at night and everything was pitch black because there was no electricity, yet the streets were filled with people who had nothing to do. As we walked along these corridors, all we could see were shining eyeballs staring back at us.

Then there was the stench. Because there was no plumbing, these corridors served as the locals' toilets and urinals. So we followed our security guards as they cut through people's makeshift houses, houses that didn't even have doors, just curtains to provide some semblance of privacy. Finally, at the end of the maze, we got to the voodoo church.

There was one huge room where the ceremony would take place. Abutting this was a series of small rooms. I walked into one of those rooms and was almost overpowered by the odor of a mountain of headless, decomposing chicken bodies—the debris of many animal offerings. I stumbled out, went to the next room, and saw a pile of kids sleeping on the floor.

The main room had colorful religious symbols painted on all the walls. We set up our generators and lights as the worshipers filed in. By the time the voodoo ceremony started, the temperature in that room had to be at least 120 degrees. Then I saw the human

(top) *Port-au-Prince, Haiti*
(bottom) *The voodoo ceremony*

CARIBBEAN SEA

Caracas

VENEZUELA

Orinoco River

Orinoco Delta

GUYANA

COLUMBIA

Puerto Ayacucho

river creates a border with Columbia

missionary complex

BRAZIL

The shrunken heads of a man and his wife

skulls and the full skeleton. The ceremony began, and it was the most intense experience I'd ever had in my life. The heat, the music, the chanting, the stench of decaying flesh—it was otherworldly. People got up and drank some kind of potion, and all of a sudden their eyes rolled back in their head, they broke into some weird ecstatic dance, and then they fell down in a trance. Around this time a small casket containing a dead child was brought out. It was paraded around the room in some kind of bizarre funeral procession.

Kalush and the other producers wanted me to do some magic during this ceremony, but I couldn't—I felt totally powerless. I didn't even have the strength to get up from my seat. At one point I couldn't feel my hands. The ceremony dragged on for over six hours—the most unbearable odor was in the room. When we finally went back to our hotel it was dawn and I felt totally drained, but I couldn't sleep. I'll never get that image of that little kid in the casket out of my mind.

We shot around Port-au-Prince for the next few days, but it wasn't easy. Magic is very real to the Haitians, and it has sinister connotations. As much as I tried to explain that what I was doing was entertainment, not real magic, they weren't buying it. I'd start to do an effect, and the Haitians would run away screaming, "This is evil. This is evil."

After a few days of being shepherded around by our guides, I was beginning to feel a little claustrophobic. So when our security was delayed one morning, I grabbed our driver. He didn't speak any English, but we directed him by pointing the way away from the usual route. We wanted to go somewhere off the beaten track. By instinct, we ended up in this really amazing area, a back road in a farming community in the hills near Port-au-Prince. People were walking around in their underwear on the dirt roads. Chickens ran around unfettered. It was a wild scene. We set up our equipment, then I grabbed a wandering chicken, ready to do the famous Dedi decapitation effect. As soon as I pulled the head off the chicken, everyone started running away from me. I wanted them to see me restore the chicken's head, so I started running toward them with the chicken's body under my arm and the head in my hand.

All of a sudden, about sixty local guys materialized from the sides of the road and started charging at us, each of them holding rocks the size of cantaloupes. They could easily have killed us and nobody would have ever known the difference, but they were just intent on scaring us away. They did a good job too. We grabbed whatever gear we could, jumped into the back of our truck, and beat it out of there.

Compared with Haiti, doing magic for the Yanomamo Indians of the Venezuelan rain forest was a walk in the park, but we had no idea what kind of reception we'd face when we flew into Puerto Ayacucho to travel to the home of this primitive tribe. I had originally wanted to do magic for the Jivaro Indians of Ecuador. The Jivaros are among the most feared headhunters of all time. To make matters worse, they're also headshrinkers, probably the last ones in the world. They're the only tribe that resisted the Spanish conquistadors; in fact, when the Spaniards sent fourteen thousand men to conquer them, the Jivaros slaughtered them all. By age ten a Jivaro would already have his first head on his belt. They'd use poison darts to kill their prey, pull the skull out of the head, and then shrink the head in a concoction of boiling herbs. They'd shrink the whole body if they had it, but they usually raided villages too far away so, for convenience's sake, they'd bring just the heads back.

In the rain forest

With the exception of Kalush, none of our producers wanted to risk a trip to Jivaros, so we compromised and decided to visit the Yanomamo territory. The Yanomamo civilization was first found in the 1970s, one of the last unknown cultures to be discovered on earth. We had been warned by a scholar not to make the trip because, he said, the Yanomami also had a penchant for attacking outsiders with darts, but we disregarded his warning. We later found out that *he* had been attacked by the Yanomami because he had aligned himself with multinational corporations that were raping the natives' land.

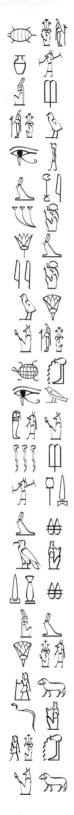

Even though we weren't going into headhunter territory, none of my producers from ABC wanted to make the trip, but one of them did offer to set me up with a Venezuelan TV producer who was living in New York. So Bill and I; our cameraman, Will; our soundman, Brad; one of my best childhood friends; and the Venezuelan producer flew into Caracas. In Caracas we changed to a small plane for the two-hour flight to Puerto Ayacucho, the last town before the rain forest. Puerto Ayacucho was like the Wild West, the end of the frontier. The best hotel in town didn't have any running water. We hadn't showered for a few days by then, but that didn't bother us. What was really irritating was the superabundance of bugs, especially the mosquitoes and gnats.

Our tour guide was almost as irritating as the insects. One of the ABC producers back in New York knew this local guide named Juan Carlos. One look at him and we realized that we were about to entrust our lives to the sketchiest guy we had ever seen. Before we set off for the rain forest, Juan Carlos recommended that we buy a variety of supplies to present to the Yanomami as goodwill gifts. Kalush was all set to buy the goods, but Juan Carlos insisted that he could purchase them more easily. So Kalush gave him about five hundred dollars cash, and he went off. Later that morning we went to board the planes and saw a whole pallet stacked with boxes out on the runway. A few minutes later a plane landed, and the airport staff began to load all this stuff onto it, so we figured we were set to go. It turned out that it wasn't our plane. When our plane finally came, they loaded on five pieces of red cloth, a dozen shotgun shells, and six machetes. Juan Carlos had totally scammed us.

Now I was getting suspicious. Again I asked Juan Carlos if he was sure that the Yanomami were expecting us, and he just smiled and nodded. So we piled into four tiny single-engine planes and took off. We flew for hours, and there wasn't a house (or a landing strip) to be seen, just lush, beautiful rain forest. After four hours in the air, we landed at a missionary complex at the base of the Orinoco River. It was weird to see a semblance of civilization right in the middle of the rain forest. The American missionaries had their own generators, running water, nice houses, even cement basketball courts. But after a few minutes, I began to get restless and turned off by these missionaries, who were there for the express purpose of converting the Indian tribes to Christianity. I was also a little upset because, as

soon as I got to the complex, I noticed a cluster of red dots on my wrists. They turned out to be gnat bites, and soon my entire body was covered with them. The missionaries administered some salve that was so corrosive it was probably worse for me than the bites themselves.

It was finally time to go downriver. We piled into the scariest-looking boat I'd ever seen. Even with all our equipment on board, it seemed that if one of us sneezed the entire boat would flip over. The boat ride seemed to last forever but, luckily enough, we didn't see

any alligators or piranhas and, because it was daytime, there were no mosquitoes to worry about. During the entire ride I was asking the Venezuelan producer and Juan Carlos questions about the Yanomami, and they both came off as expert cultural anthropologists.

After a good eight hours, we approached the Yanomamo village. That's when Juan Carlos finally admitted that he had never been to *this* Yanomamo village, but he reassured us that they were definitely expecting us. I shot a glance at Kalush. Picking up on my concern, the Venezuelan producer told us not to worry, he would speak Spanish to the Yanomami and straighten everything out. The only problem was the Yanomami don't speak Spanish.

Judging from the puzzled stares we got from the locals as we disembarked, they had no idea we were coming to visit them. We had landed at a very small village; their entire territory was about a quarter the size of a New York City block. There were at most thirty people in the village. It was also literally a small village because the Yanomami were really tiny. Besides being tiny, they all looked like they were about seventy years old, even though the great majority of them were in their twenties. Most of them walked around naked, which was practical since it was about 120 degrees at midday, but some of them had underwear on.

I took a quick look around. There were a few straw huts. I saw some pots and pans. There was a big soccer square. A volleyball net. A little kid had one roller skate. I guessed that the missionaries had been here once or twice. I was certain when I saw one very light-skinned Yanomamo baby.

We walked into the village, and a few of the elders warily approached us. Even though they didn't speak Spanish, one Yanomamo knew a few Spanish phrases, and somehow Juan Carlos was able to communicate to them that I was the shaman of our group. Comprehending, the Indians led us to this closed hut. Inside, a number of men were sitting around a circle, telling

Magic in the middle of the jungle

stories and inhaling a powerful native psychedelic called yoco.

One Indian would stand up and do a long, beautiful-sounding oration. Meanwhile, another native squatted on the ground, grinding this tree bark on a stone. While he was doing that he was stomping his feet and pacing back and forth in a small circle. Then another native took the residue from the tree bark and packed it into the end of a long bamboo shoot. He put the bamboo shoot into another Indian's nostril and, *wham,* blew the yoco right up the guy's nose. The native's head snapped back like he'd been shot, his eyes watered, and then this black blood began oozing out of his nose and mouth. He started hacking and spitting up blood-infused mucus, and then he just leaned back as the substance kicked in. He was in Yanomamo never-never land. The women and children were in the same hut, but they weren't allowed to talk or even get near the sacred circle.

So this was the scene we walked into. Since it was so unlike anything we had ever seen before, we all just watched quietly until the shaman of the tribe walked up to me and offered me some of the psychedelic. I didn't want to do it, but I thought I should show them something strong, so I put my hands to my mouth and starting coughing. A shower of Venezuelan coins rained out of my mouth. The Indians knew the coins were valuable, but they wouldn't touch them. I guess they figured that I might transfer diseases to them, or maybe they felt there was something evil in the coin effect. Whatever it was, someone first had to wash the coins and then do a little ceremony over them before they gathered some leaves and gingerly picked up the coins with them.

After producing the coins, I took a leaf off a tree and a dead fish fell out of the leaf. The Yanomami looked impressed. Then they looked toward their shaman. I later found out that he was their shaman because he was capable of taking the most hits off that bamboo shoot. The shaman looked right at me and, without warning, started making these choking sounds. The next thing I knew he

Replicating Dedi's four-thousand-year-old feat in Manhattan. Next time I'll do it with a polar bear.

was pulling a huge piece of glass out of his mouth, a piece much bigger than his mouth. He wasn't through. He started hacking away again and produced what looked to be a huge slab of his liver from his mouth. I was shocked. Here we were in the middle of nowhere, and the leader of their tribe was doing magic effects to me.

By then it was almost dark, and since there was no electricity in the village, everyone went to bed with the sun's departure. I had a feeling that, despite my magic and my newfound bond with their shaman, they were still a little wary of us. That was reinforced when they put us up for the night in the tribe's slaughterhouse. For two nights we slept in this foul-smelling hut until we complained so much that they moved us to a makeshift shelter on the other side of the village. There were no walls here, just a bunch of poles and a thatched roof, so when it rained, the rain poured right onto us. We set up hammocks between the trees. We had long nets that went right to the ground so we wouldn't get any nocturnal visits from the local scorpions, tarantulas, or snakes, but the first night I was so woozy from the travel I didn't notice that my net was inches from the ground at one spot. The next morning I woke up with 282 mosquito bites on one arm alone. I knew it was that many; I counted each one.

There wasn't much else to do. The villagers absolutely refused to allow us to film me doing magic to them. They'd made that clear from the minute we arrived. The Yanomami felt that the cameras would suck their souls away. Then they looked at the presents Juan Carlos had insisted we bring and said, "We thank you for the shotgun shells and the machetes and the red cloth, but we don't really want them." Maybe we should have brought them the other roller skate. One thing they did seem to like was my playing cards. I handed a playing card to one villager, and he just stared at it for two hours. I'm sure the psychedelics had something to do with that.

In general, there wasn't much there for anyone to do. Once a young man builds his hut and becomes an adult, there's really no work for him for the rest of his life. They don't need water because they have the great river. There are so many fish that we saw buck-naked kids standing on the banks of the river spearing fish at will. They don't need agriculture because they can just stroll into the jungle and pick the most amazing-tasting fruit right off the trees.

There's one guy who has a job, though. Since they can't read and they have no written language (and no light to read in bed anyway), as soon as it's dark, everything stops. Then, with the first light, this guy runs around to each hut and does a whistle song to wake everyone up. So they can sit around all day and do nothing.

By the third day I realized that our lives were in the hands of that sketchy tour guide Juan Carlos. After we disembarked from the boat, it left. We had already paid for the round-trip boat ride in advance, so if for any reason the captain forgot to return to get us, we'd never get back to civilization. Nobody else knew exactly where we were since there are thousands of tiny Yanomamo villages. If the captain decided to blow us off, we'd most likely soon be dead from some horrible tropical disease like malaria. I was certain that I'd already caught malaria after I woke up with those hundreds of mosquito bites, especially since I had neglected to take the malaria pills we were given back in New York. When I heard that two people in that village had come down with the disease and were on their last legs, I was certain I was a goner.

Despite my paranoia, there was nothing we could do, so we ate our supplies and used Kalush's pump to purify the river water. We had depleted our own water supply the first day because of the unrelenting heat. On top of that, I was wearing all black—black slacks and a black cashmere sweater—in the 120-degree heat. I wasn't turning out to be much of a shaman.

After a week it seemed that the Yanomami were warming up to us a little bit. I had been doing some magic for the kids, who were

The Yanomamo village seen from the air

fascinated by these alien visitors. Whenever we were in our hut, all the children would gather outside and just stare at us. Then one of the elders would yell something and the kids would scatter.

On the seventh day we were there, they finally let us use the cameras. We were allowed to shoot for exactly one hour. That afternoon we had an inkling that something was up, because the whole village suddenly disappeared. Nobody was playing volleyball. Nobody was fishing. Nobody was staring at us. They were all gone. Then, one hour later, the entire village came out of the ceremonial hut and walked toward us. Instead of wearing loincloths or underwear, they were garbed in their colorful ornamental outfits, made up with elaborate makeup, and carrying ceremonial spears. We pulled the cameras out, and nobody objected.

I did a succession of effects for them, and the Yanomami loved the magic. They were really sweet, but after an hour an elder walked up and stopped the shooting. I was amazed that we finally had something to show for our journey, and I didn't want to overstay our welcome, but we had to wait three more days for the boat to arrive.

The original plan was for the boat to take us downriver to another Yanomamo village, and it did. The captain told us that this new village was sheltered and protected, and we wouldn't have to sleep tied between trees. We needed something like that. By then we could barely walk, we had so little energy left. Except for a few crackers, we were totally out of food. We had no water. I hadn't bathed for over a week because I was afraid that if I went in the river the piranhas might get me. The only problem was that this new village was a thousand times more horrifying than the first one. These villagers also had no idea that we were coming, and our luxurious accommodations turned out to be a hut that reeked from the odor of the dog carcasses that littered the village. This village was even poorer than the first one. The only signs of civilization here were two huge posters of Brad Pitt and Leonardo Di Caprio that hung in one of the decrepit huts. That was it. It was time to head home.

We piled back into the boat. The captain wanted to go on to another village, but we overruled him and forced him to take us back. The missionary camp that I couldn't tolerate a week ago now looked like a five-star hotel. One of the missionaries let us crash on her kitchen floor. Sleeping on a floor was heaven compared with being strung up on a hammock tied between two trees, with a net that allowed every gnat, bug, mosquito, and spider to crawl all over you. Before we crashed the missionary gave us all something to drink. I normally don't drink soda, but that refrigerated Coke tasted like the greatest thing in the world. After a few days the planes finally showed up, and we headed home.

Being back in New York never felt so good. Between the U.S. shoots, Haiti, and the Yanomami, we had compelling footage for my second TV special, but I realized that, even though performing street magic was great, I had always wanted to do something really spectacular. Exactly a hundred years earlier, in the spring of 1899, a magician had amazed people by staging his first massive outdoor stunts. I decided it was time for me to do my first big stunt. All I had to do was refine my ideas. For that I went back to my first books on magic and reacquainted myself with the life and times of one of the greatest performers who ever lived.

The Karma Fountain Test

Here's a simple little test to determine how good your karma is. Just by following my directions you can learn whether you're emitting a positive aura or a negative one. You'll need the big coin jar that you throw all your spare change into. If you don't have one, or if it's empty, grab a pile of change. Make sure you have a good number of pennies, nickels, dimes, and quarters.

For this test, silver denotes a positive karma, and your nickels, dimes, and quarters represent it. Copper denotes a negative karmic value, which is represented by the pennies. When you throw coins into a fountain, you hope to affect your karma, so for this experiment I need you to make a makeshift fountain. Take a napkin in your left hand and hold it by gathering its four corners together. Make sure there's some room to put coins into the napkin. (See illustration.)

Now we need to throw some coins into our napkin fountain. This step

relies on your personal experiences, so while you follow my instructions, I want you to recall your own unique memories.

Think of a time when you

- Gave a homeless person a friendly smile. Put three silver coins into the napkin.
- Walked by a homeless person and pretended not to see them. Put three pennies into the napkin.
- Let others maliciously gossip about a friend of yours. Put one penny in the napkin.
- Cut in line. Put one penny in the napkin.
- Admitted you did something wrong, even though you didn't have to. Put three silver coins in the napkin.
- Helped a complete stranger with something. Throw four silvers in the napkin.
- Ignored a loved one. Throw two pennies in the napkin.
- Lied or cheated. Put four pennies in the napkin.
- Tormented your brother, sister, or a friend. Throw two pennies in the napkin.
- Did something kind for a loved one. Throw two silver coins in the napkin.
- Stole something instead of earning it. Put five pennies in the napkin.
- Returned a valuable item that someone else lost. Put five silver coins in the napkin.
- Said good morning to a complete stranger. Throw two silver coins in the napkin.
- Betrayed a confidence. Put two pennies in the napkin.
- Ate healthy food instead of junk food. Throw one silver coin in.
- Conserved water or energy without being reminded. Throw four silvers in the napkin.
- Didn't try to do your best. Put two pennies in the napkin.
- Tried to do your very best. Throw two silvers in the napkin.

Now I'm going to assess your own unique karma. When I ask you to pull out

coins, I want you to reach with your right hand into the fountain (napkin) and take out two coins. These can only be two silvers, two coppers, or one of each. You shouldn't think about which coins you might be taking, just grab two at random. Your individual life karma will guide which coins you remove and thus determine the outcome.

First I want you to recall a memory from any time in your life that was decidedly unpleasant. Now reach into the napkin and pull out two coins. If they are both silver coins, start a pile on the table to the left, if they are both copper, start a pile on the right. If they are one of each, they negate each other's karma so just discard them into your original coin jar. We won't need them again. Now recall a different memory, one that was pleasant and makes you feel warm all over. Again pull out two coins at random and put the coins in their correct places as instructed above.

Continue this, alternating bad and good memories. I know this might be painful, but it's important that you remember strong memories, things that really affected your psyche sometime in your life. Keep pulling out two coins at a time until there are no coins left in your makeshift fountain. You can put the napkin aside now. You should now have two piles of coins in front of you—one all silver, one all copper. I have no idea how many coins are in each pile. Now I want you to add up the number of coins (not their monetary value) in each pile, as this is going to indicate your relative karma. If you have more silver coins than copper you have a positive karmic value. If the two piles are equal, you are perfectly balanced at this point in your life. If you have more copper coins than silver ones, it's an indication that your karma needs some work.

Remember, the publisher allowed us to print up many different versions of this book. It's no coincidence that you happened to buy this particular version. In fact, you could say that that action itself was karmically determined, because I know that you pulled four more silver coins from the napkin than copper ones, which tells me that your karma is very positive. You should be very happy with this outcome and I hope that your future actions increase the positive value of your karma.

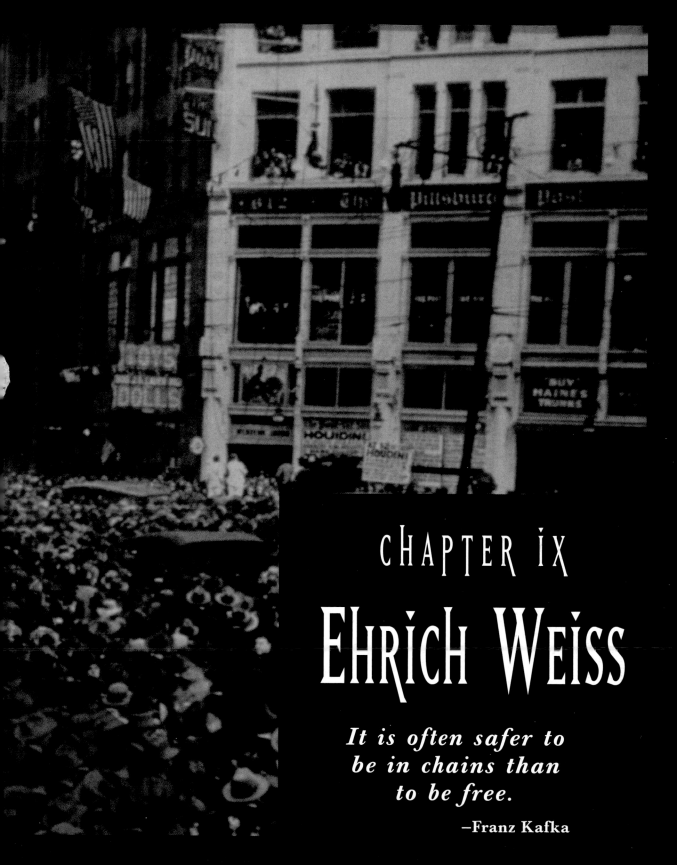

CHAPTER IX

EHRICH WEISS

*It is often safer to
be in chains than
to be free.*

—Franz Kafka

Ehrich Weiss

He escaped from a straitjacket while dangling head first two hundred feet above the amazed onlookers in Piccadilly Circus. He jumped into the Thames River from Westminster Bridge sporting six pairs of leg irons, eight pairs of handcuffs, twenty-five feet of chain and, for good measure, eight padlocks. Secured in another straitjacket, he was thrown into a cage full of lions. He once was handcuffed, locked into a mailbag, and dropped into the water from a low-flying aircraft. He survived. He claimed to be the world's greatest escapologist.

His name was . . . Murray.

Today, except for a few magic history scholars, no one remembers Murray. Even fewer people remember Hourdene, Whodini, Cutini, and Stillini—all performers who imitated and traded off the name of the most famous magician who ever lived, a man who was said by George Bernard Shaw to be among the three best-known names in history—Jesus Christ and Sherlock Holmes being the other two. That man, of course, was Houdini.

More than seventy-five years after his death, his name still resonates around the world. Why do we still care about Houdini? I think part of the answer is that Houdini, while he was still alive, created a conviction in the minds of his audience that he was much more than a mere magician. Although he harbored a lifelong dream to do a big illusion-filled evening of traditional magic (and he failed twice before succeeding in the year before his death), the biggest illusion Houdini created was his own myth—that he was one man who could not be contained. Whether it was by handcuffs or straitjackets, armored vehicles or water-filled torture cells, Houdini could escape with his life. It was the myth of a modern-day Superman. In the end, that same myth probably killed him.

Ehrich Weiss was an improbable hero. He was born in Budapest on March 24, 1874, the third of five sons of Mayer Samuel Weiss and his wife, Cecilia. When Ehrich was two his father emi-

grated to America. Two years later Mayer Weiss obtained a job as the rabbi of a small congregation in Appleton, Wisconsin, and sent for his family. The early years in America were not kind to the young Ehrich. After the family had been in Appleton for a few years, the congregation fired Mayer and hired a younger, more progressive rabbi. The Weisses then tottered on the brink of poverty as Mayer remained unemployed. By the time he left for New York to search for work, his wife had given birth to another son and a daughter.

Ehrich seemed special from the beginning. As an infant he hardly slept—his inquisitive eyes were always staring at the walls of the bedroom. He seemed to have a sense of responsibility that transcended his tender age. After Mayer's eldest son died at age twenty-two, the rabbi, sick with grief, called his remaining sons around him and made them promise to take care of their mother if anything should happen to him. Ehrich took this oath to heart and, even though he was only twelve, left home intent on earning money for the family. After a year on the road, he met up with his father in New York and got a job as a uniformed messenger for a department store. With his son's supplemental income, the rabbi was able to reunite the family in New York.

They still struggled. Rabbi Weiss was reduced to working side by side with his son at a necktie factory. It was here that Ehrich developed his fascination with magic. He started buying magic books and discovered that his co-worker Jacob Hyman was also an enthusiast. Along with doing magic Ehrich devoted his spare time to athletics, mainly swimming and running—perhaps hoping to strengthen his body so he wouldn't succumb to tuberculosis, the way his older half brother had. In 1889 he began performing magic at small social functions, using the name Ehrich the Great.

On one of his forays for used magic books, he stumbled upon *The Memoirs of Robert-Houdin*, and the French magician instantly became his hero. By the end of March 1891, Ehrich and Jacob had quit their jobs and teamed up to do magic. Under the mistaken impression that when the letter *i* was added to a name in French,

EAST E.E.

it meant "like," they called themselves the Brothers Houdini.

What gave young Harry (the Americanized version of his nickname, Ehrie) Houdini the idea that he could fulfill his father's injunction to look after his mother by quitting a respectable job and becoming a magician? Perhaps it was the séance Ehrich attended with his old friend Joe Rinn. The two boys, along with about forty others, paid a buck apiece to watch a fat medium named Minnie Williams conjure up a host of spirits. Houdini saw right through Minnie's scams (recognizing the male "spirit" as the medium herself in drag), but he was impressed enough to whisper to Rinn, "There must be plenty of money in this game."

Around this time Harry read *Revelations of a Spirit Medium*—a tell-all book that described how mediums created bogus spirit manifestations under the cover of darkness by releasing themselves after being bound with rope. Soon after reading it Harry, his brother Theo, and Rinn were taking turns escaping from rope ties with amazing speed.

Bess Houdini, distraught after her husband's death. She later opened a bar.

The Brothers Houdini debuted their act in the spring of 1893 at a dime museum in New York City. Dime museums were at the lowest rung of showbiz (only seedy beer halls were lower), and the Brothers Houdini performed twenty times a day on the curio stage, which they shared with the leading freaks of the time. After knocking around the circuit for a year, Jacob dissolved their partnership. Jacob's brother filled in for a few weeks until Harry enlisted his real younger brother Theo in May 1894. Theo, bigger than Harry (who, according to his first passport, was only five foot four), didn't last long in the act. While working in Coney Island, he met Wilhelmina Beatrice Rahner, who was part of a song-and-dance act named the Floral Sisters. She was less than five feet tall and weighed only ninety pounds. Wilhelmina had run away from home and changed her name to Bess Raymond to pursue a frowned-upon showbiz career. Theo introduced Bess to Harry. Within weeks Harry and Bess had married, and now it was Bess who wound up in the act instead of Theo.

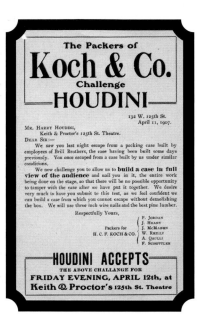

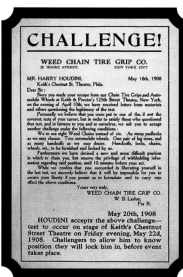

The Houdinis hit the road. For the next five years they criss-crossed the country with little more than a dream of making it to the big time. They played beer halls and dime museums. They even worked with a traveling circus, where Harry supplemented their meager income by selling soap and toothpaste to the other performers. When their magic act failed to sustain them, the Houdinis took whatever work they could scrape up. They performed both as a comedy team and in a melodrama. Harry worked as the card magician Cardo and as Dr. Murat, a hypnotist. In the winter of 1897, Bessie and Harry joined up with Dr. Hill's California Concert Company, a traveling medicine show. In Kansas, "Dr." Hill offered Harry top billing if he and Bess would do a Sunday night spirit séance. Using confederates as tipsters and visiting local cemeteries for family histories, Harry put together a phony medium act that astounded the audience.

Bookings were scarce, so Harry and Bessie struggled on. Whenever they made some money, Harry would put away enough for their expenses and send the rest home to his mom, who was now widowed. At one point he and his wife subsisted on potatoes alone. While some people might have bemoaned their fate, Houdini savored every experience on the road, prying trade secrets out of every old performer he'd meet. He learned an amazing needle-swallowing effect from Maxey, the Human Sewing Machine, in a dime museum in Lynn, Massachusetts. While with the circus he learned to swallow and regurgitate objects—a talent that would come in handy in his later handcuff escapes. During the same circus stint, he literally learned at the feet of Lutes, the Armless Wonder, a sideshow freak who taught Houdini how to use his toes as fingers.

Inspiration was everywhere. When Harry ripped apart an old packing crate to burn for firewood, he got an idea for an escape. When he toured an insane asylum in New Brunswick, he came upon an inmate struggling to escape from a straitjacket. The sight intrigued him, and soon he had worked out a straitjacket escape.

Unlike Minnie the Medium, though, Harry still wasn't making money. Times got so bad that he and Bess returned to New York in 1898 and moved in with his mother. Desperate for money, Harry tried to sell off all his effects. He prepared a sixteen-page catalog called "Magic Made Easy" by Professor Harry Houdini—King of Cards and Handcuffs. One ad featured a drawing of a blindfolded medium with an angel with flowing wings whispering in her ear.

I give Scyerometric and Clairvoyantic Readings, telling you the Past, Present and Future. I will tell you your innermost secrets. Satisfaction guaranteed!! And I not not ask any questions! Can learn anyone. TERMS, Moderate.

Do you believe in Spiritualism? If not, why not? If you want to give Manifestations or Slate Tests I can give you full instructions and make you a full fledged medium! Write for particulars.

HARRY HOUDINI, 221 E. 69th Street, New York City.

Professor Harry Houdini's magic catalog

Despite such wonderful ad copy, Harry made few sales. He was about to give up show business for good, but he had some earlier contracts to fulfill. The Houdinis were working in a beer hall in Minnesota in the spring of 1899 when Martin Beck, a prominent booker for the vaudeville circuit, challenged Harry to escape from a pair of handcuffs. Harry, who had been doing challenge escapes for several years, defeated Beck's cuffs. Impressed, Beck booked him. Suddenly Dime Museum Harry was touring the vaudeville circuit with a ten-to-thirty-minute act, appearing only twice a day. In a short time his salary increased from twenty-five dollars a week to ten times that amount.

Harry learned a lot under Beck's tutelage. The agent helped him polish his presentation but, more important, he streamlined the act to emphasize the escapes rather than the magic. Escape acts were not new. Colorni had done rope escapes in the sixteenth century. Pinetti had escaped from ropes and chains in the 1700s. A French magician, La Tude, did a handcuff escape as early as 1700. Samri Baldwin, "the White Mahatma," did handcuff escapes in

the context of spiritualist séances in New Orleans in the 1870s.

Joe Godfrey, Louis Paul, and a midget named Zamora all had escaped from cuffs years before. But Houdini was one of the first to introduce the notion of a challenge—escaping from any cuffs the audience would supply. (Although he quickly learned that he must first inspect them to be sure they were in working order. While working in Chicago in January 1899, he accepted handcuffs from a cop named Waldron. After an hour Houdini was still cuffed and the audience had filtered out. Waldron then gleefully told Houdini that the cuffs were plugged and couldn't be opened. That night a distraught Houdini was convinced that his career was over.)

On the vaudeville circuit, Harry brilliantly worked the press to publicize his shows. When he hit a new town, he invited reporters to the local jail, where lunch and some liquid refreshments were served. Then the police would cuff him and lock him into a cell. Within minutes Harry would escape. The police would sign an affidavit, and the grateful, well-fed and -fueled press would write breathless stories. After a year in vaudeville, Houdini was making four hundred dollars a week, almost 80 percent of the *annual* salary of an average American laborer.

A mishap in New York proved to be another fortuitous event in the continuing education of Harry. At the beginning of February 1900, during their run in the New York Theatre, the Houdinis performed their signature effect, a trunk substitution. Harry's hands were bound, and he was secured in a silk bag, then locked in a trunk. Bess then closed a curtain, clapped her hands, and within seconds Harry emerged from behind the curtain and opened the trunk, to reveal a bound Bess. That night Harry bounced out from behind the curtain and, flashing his famous smile, bent over to unlock the trunk to free Bess but realized he had forgotten the key. A search of the dressing room proved futile. By now Bess was beating her fists against the inside of the trunk, screaming, so the stage manager started to wield a fire ax. Then an assistant rushed up with the key. Bess, who had fainted, was carried to her dressing room.

Thanks to the press coverage of this mishap, the rest of the shows sold out. The lesson wasn't lost on Harry. From then on he was acutely aware that the element of danger in the escapes could increase both the audience's size and their involvement in the ongoing drama. For a long time he had fallen into the trap of demonstrating his cleverness and skill by making his escapes look *easy.*

The drama, he realized, would come from making them look *hard*.

With this lesson under his belt, Harry and Bess set sail to conquer Europe on May 30, 1900. In London, Harry dragged the manager of the Alhambra Theatre to Scotland Yard to demonstrate his facility for escapes. On arriving the manager told the inspector, "I think this fellow is crazy—lock him up for a while." The cop grabbed Harry and handcuffed him to a pole. "That's the way we lock 'em up over here," he said smugly. Seconds later Harry threw the cuffs to the ground. "This is the way we get out of them in America."

Houdini became an overnight sensation in England and on the Continent by following a very simple formula: hit a city, do a jailbreak, get publicity, sell out shows. When he arrived in Germany, he added a sensational publicity-generating device: he began a series of daredevil dives into rivers while manacled. (When he returned to America years later, twenty thousand people thronged the Steel Pier at Atlantic City to watch him do it there.)

Houdini right before he was padlocked, secured in a packing crate, and dumped into New York Harbor, 1914

The bridge jumps and jailbreaks were not the only means he used to promote his shows. Houdini was perhaps the most publicity-savvy entertainer ever, and he was constantly coming up with new ways to promote himself. In Paris he hired seven men in bowler hats to sit together. On cue the seven would pull their hats off and reveal bald heads, each with a single letter on it. Together the heads spelled HOUDINI. Houdini plastered England with over 36,000 advertising sheets. In every country he ran full-page newspaper ads trumpeting his name in huge, bold letters. He issued a promotional booklet in the shape of a lock. He sold (or gave away) a series of pitch books that, by 1922, totaled 6 million copies. He told a friend that he spent "every cent I could spare in advertising myself." Another friend wasn't so charitable. "Houdini would murder his grandmother for publicity," he said.

Houdini even did product endorsements ("Houdini uses Zam-Buk [lotion] for cuts, bruises, and sores"). He patented a windup doll that stood upside down on its flat head and escaped from a straitjacket. When ticket sales for one of his German shows lagged in December 1908, he went out on the streets and passed out the handbills himself.

Houdini escapes from a straitjacket in 1906.

His drive to succeed bordered on the obsessive. When he arrived in Europe in 1900, he was immediately confronted with other escape artists who attempted to "expose" the upstart American as a fraud. Houdini became obsessed with his "imitators" and took an almost sadistic pleasure in destroying his competition. (Literally too. If we are to believe his brother Theo, Harry was once so upset at a circus escapologist who claimed to be greater than he was but would never accept a challenge that Harry set fire to the structure where his rival's act was being exhibited. He later said he regretted having done so because "innocent jungle beasts might have been destroyed.")

After a few months in Europe, Harry summoned his brother. (COME OVER. THE APPLES ARE RIPE, he cabled.) Afraid that a horde of less-than-proficient imitators would sour the public on the whole escape game, he set his brother up as his principal rival. By the time

Theo reached Berlin, Harry had his act plotted out—settings, handcuffs, a substitution trunk, a girl assistant, even a name. At first he planned to name his brother Hardeeni but, fearing it was too close to his own name, he settled on Hardeen. For the next fifteen years the two brothers, while acknowledging their common ancestry, feigned a grudge feud and crisscrossed the world in supposed competition. "The newspapers having us cutting each other's throats—and just two loving brothers living off the fat of the land," Hardeen gleefully recounted.

Houdini often disrupted the acts of his imitators and dramatically handcuffed them onstage. When they couldn't escape, Houdini would let them rot in their bondage, at least until the press came to document his victory. Pitched stage battles like these might seem fantastic to today's reader, but they serve to illuminate a central facet of Houdini's appeal—the emotional component in his performance. Most stage magicians at the time were presenting extravagant shows featuring full-scale illusions that would momentarily delight the audience, but Houdini touched his audience in a much more profound way. By escaping bondage in any of its various forms, sometimes at the hands of agents of the state, Houdini was an inspiration to all those who yearned for freedom from oppression. It was not a coincidence that he initially enjoyed his greatest popularity in countries that had the most totalitarian regimes—Germany and Russia.

After Bess's near tragedy in the trunk, Harry had honed the dramatic nature of his escapes. "The secret of showmanship consists of not what you really do, but what the mystery-loving public *thinks* you do," he wrote. He had as many as five full-time assistants, whose job was to make sure that he could successfully and safely escape from any challenge or stunt. His shackled bridge jumps looked incredibly dangerous, but every precaution was taken to ensure Houdini's safety. "The problem wasn't in releasing ourselves from the cuffs after we were in the water," Hardeen revealed years later. "The problem was keeping the cuffs on until we hit the water." Even so, Houdini would have a safety rope attached to him before he jumped and an assistant who served as a saver, ready to jump into the water at a moment's notice.

A consummate showman, Houdini commanded a stage. His mastery over an audience and impressive ability to think on his feet were best demonstrated on December 1, 1915, at the Orpheum Theatre in Los Angeles. He had called for the usual committee of

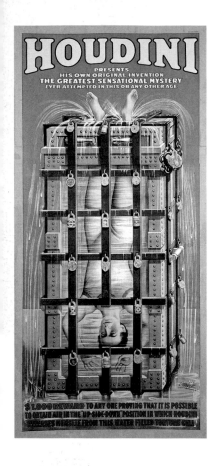

ten observers to come onstage, but only seven people had volunteered. Then Houdini spotted Jess Willard, the newly crowned heavyweight champion of the world, in the audience. Noting that "he will be enough for three ordinary gentlemen," Houdini introduced Willard and invited him onstage. The audience gave Willard an ovation, but Willard refused.

"Aw, g'wan with your act." The champ glowered at Houdini. "Give me the same wages you pay those other fellows and I'll come down." The audience fell silent. "All right," Houdini said. "I'll pay you what I pay these seven men. Kindly step right down and come onstage." Of course, Houdini paid the volunteers nothing.

Willard rose to his feet. "Go on wid the show, you faker. Everyone knows you're a four-flusher." The audience started hissing. Houdini raised his hand to quiet them, walked down to the footlights and, white with rage, addressed Willard. "Look here, you. I don't care how big you are or who you are. I paid you a compliment when I asked you to be on the committee. You have the right to refuse, but you have no right to slur my reputation. Let me tell you one thing, and don't forget this, that *I will be Harry Houdini when you are not the heavyweight champion of the world.*" The audience cheered Houdini and booed Willard out of the theater. The incident made the front pages of every newspaper in America.

There are numerous stories of Houdini being mobbed after a show and paraded on the shoulders of his fans back to his hotel, where they refused to leave until he addressed them. And why not? Houdini was the Self-Liberator, able to escape from any confinement challenge hurled his way. Over the next fifteen years he would escape from a U.S. mail pouch, a sealed coffin, a giant envelope, a giant football (carried onstage by the University of Pennsylvania football team), heavy automobile chains, a glass box, a man-sized sausage skin, to name only a few. Nothing could hold him.

When handcuff escapes were no longer novel and his audiences started shrinking, Houdini introduced a new escape—from a water-filled, heavily padlocked milk can. Once the milk can escape started being utilized by competitors, Houdini designed and built what many people feel was his most amazing escape effect, the Chinese Water Torture Cell, a cabinet built exactly to Houdini's height that was filled with water. To some it resembled a glass phone booth. Houdini was secured in handcuffs and ankle bracelets, then hoisted upside down and inserted into the water headfirst. The cabinet was

locked, the curtain drawn, and two and half minutes later the curtain would part and Houdini would appear, dripping wet but free. Although this stunt looked exceedingly dangerous, it was so well engineered that the risks were minimal.

In addition to his amazing escapes on the stage, Houdini would continually perform free outdoor stunts. The most famous of these were the straitjacket escapes, which were probably the most dangerous stunts he ever performed. Suspended by his feet from a crane or a flagpole jutting off a tall building, Houdini rocked violently from side to side like a man possessed until he released himself from his containment and threw the jacket to the crowd below. "Human beings don't like to see other human beings lose their lives, but they *do* love to be on the spot when it happens," Houdini noted sardonically. He was right. In April 1916 an estimated 100,000 people, the biggest crowd in D.C. history (except for a presidential inauguration), thronged the downtown streets to watch Houdini, dangling one hundred feet in the air, escape from his jacket. In Baltimore the next week, he drew 50,000 spectators for his stunt. In New York City police reported a record number of pockets picked as thousands looked up at the dangling showman.

Although all of Houdini's stunts and escapes were planned down to the minutest detail, there was always an element of danger

Houdini's Chinese Water Torture Cell

Another outdoor Houdini straitjacket escape. This was in New York City in 1916.

in their execution. On five separate occasions he broke bones. Trying to escape from a fifty-gallon cask that was filled with the finest English ale, the teetotaler was overcome by the fumes and had to be rescued by an assistant. (Never one to admit defeat, Houdini repeated this escape and succeeded by first coating his body with oil. The oil prevented absorption of the alcohol through his skin.) His most serious brush with death occurred at a Pittsburgh YMCA when Houdini did a manacled high dive into a water tank. He miscalculated the depth of the water, and his head smashed into the cement bottom of the tank, knocking him unconscious. He had to be dragged out of the water, and he sported a scar for the rest of his life.

To the master mystifier, all this went with the territory. "My chief task has been to conquer fear," he said. "The public sees only the thrill of the accomplished trick; they have no conception of the tortuous preliminary self-training that was necessary to conquer

fear. . . . No one except myself can appreciate how I have to work at this job every single day, never letting up for a moment. I always have on my mind the thought that next year I must do something greater, something more wonderful." One of Houdini's longtime assistants confirmed this obsessiveness. "Houdini was an intense man, so completely devoted to his work that he rarely thought about anything else. . . . We were continually working and Houdini thought nothing of waking us in the middle of the night to send us scurrying off for wood to build some new gimmick, or to have us wet down the hotel's bed sheets and wrap him in them to see if he could master a new escape."

To elicit a conviction in the audience's minds that you are a Superman, it's necessary to believe it yourself, to paraphrase Robert-Houdin. In November 1911, Houdini escaped from a bag in Detroit, but because a buckle had been tied too tight, he burst a blood vessel in his kidney. He bled for over two weeks before he even considered

going to a doctor, who ordered a long break from work with total bed rest. Houdini was back on the road in December.

It takes a unique man to assume this role, and Houdini was, if anything, unique. Harold Kellock, who wrote Houdini's authorized biography after his death, described him as "at once self-sufficient, quite boyishly helpless, quick-tempered, tender-hearted, stern, sentimental, sophisticated, childlike, lavish, frugal, impulsive, patient, resentful, kindly, awesomely sincere." Sir Arthur Conan Doyle, who enjoyed a tempestuous relationship with Houdini, called him "the most curious and intriguing character whom I have ever encountered."

He certainly was eccentric. When Houdini was pulling down over a thousand dollars a week performing in England, a friend found him staying at a threadbare rooming house because he liked the landlady's cooking. At other times food didn't even interest him. He'd go twelve hours without eating, then drink two quarts of milk with a dozen raw eggs stirred in them. For thirty-three years Bess dutifully washed his ears with soap and water. If she didn't do it, it would never be done. He never changed his underwear. Bess would have to spirit the soiled underwear away at night and replace it with new pairs. Once Houdini put on a suit, he'd wear it indefinitely, or at least until Bess could make a switch while he was onstage.

As one might expect, Houdini had his enemies, usually lesser magicians who seemed jealous of his success and fame. The British magician Harry Leat called him "the best hated conjurer in America." Other magicians complained that when they were in his company he would talk only about himself. Houdini did have a massive ego. He was backstage at a theater once when a fan approached to ask him to autograph one of his books. After Houdini complied, the fan recognized Joseph Dunninger, a young mentalist, and asked Dunninger to add his signature. As soon as Dunninger inscribed the page, Houdini grabbed the book and wrote the word "witness" under Dunninger's name, making it appear that Dunninger had merely authenticated Houdini's signature.

Houdini with his good friend and fellow magician Harry Kellar

Houdini could be petty, but he was amazingly generous too. He gave many benefit performances at hospitals, insane asylums, and prisons. When World War I broke out Houdini tried to enlist, but he was rejected as too old. Undeterred, he organized rallies and raised over a million dollars for the war effort. At these benefits he would magically produce gold dollar coins and bestow them on the servicemen in the audience. He gave out seven thousand dollars in coins.

Houdini had a particularly soft spot for children. He regularly performed at orphanages and even devised a unique performance for blind children. In Edinburgh, Scotland, he bought up the entire children's inventory of a local shoe store, then placed an ad in the paper offering free shoes for any child that needed them. Three hundred pairs of shoes later, there was still a long line of disappointed children, so, like a Pied Piper, Houdini marched them to another store until every child had a new pair of shoes.

Taken on Board the Hamburg American Liner "IMPERATOR" In Mid Ocean June 23. 1914.

Houdini poses with former president Theodore Roosevelt.

His generosity even extended to fellow performers (as long as they weren't escape artists). As one might imagine, Houdini was an incredibly hard act to follow. Will Rogers, the cowboy humorist, once had to do that and wrote, "I might just as well have got on my little pony and ridden back to the livery stable as to have ridden out on that stage." Cognizant of their dilemma, Houdini made it a practice to linger in the wings after he performed and cheer on the following acts—especially if they were newcomers to show business.

At the time of Houdini's death he was supporting scores of needy people—some itinerant magicians, some incapacitated friends, some vague acquaintances. Houdini's generosity to his fraternal magicians even extended beyond death. He made it a point to seek out famous magicians' graves, and if they were in disrepair he paid for perpetual care. He tried to rehabilitate the images of some of these forgotten conjurers. Soon after he toured Europe for the first time, Houdini started research for a book that would document the history of conjuring (and correct the then-standard history by Thomas Frost, an Englishman).

As he interviewed old magicians and collected data, Houdini became convinced that his boyhood idol, Robert-Houdin, had grossly overestimated his contributions to magic in his autobiography. Houdini's resultant book, *The Unmasking of Robert-Houdin,* was a vicious attack on his former mentor but perhaps in Houdini's mind an attempt to restore the rightful reputations of the forgotten magicians whose innovations he felt Robert-Houdin had taken credit for. (It is interesting that the book is dedicated to Houdini's father, a scholar who, in his son's eyes, was also never accorded the respect due him in his lifetime.) But Houdini's attempt to clarify Robert-Houdin's place in the history of magic contained countless mistakes, so it actually further muddied the waters.

Issues of respect and legitimacy became more prominent as Houdini aged. By 1909 he was resisting the appellation "magician," telling the Australian press, "Don't insult me and call me a magician. I'm an escape artist." He asked that his entry in *Who's Who in America* be amended, and under occupation he listed "actor, inventor, author," not magician.

Of course, by then he had been doing more acting than stage magic. As vaudeville waned Houdini threw himself into the new movie industry, at one point starting his own movie production company. Although the movies he made helped spread his fame, they were artistic disasters. Houdini's acting was wooden, the plots lame and predictable, and, except for one or two thrilling scenes, the films were almost unwatchable. By 1922 he had lost over half a million dollars and was forced to shut down his studio and film processing business. "*No* illusion is good in a Film, as we simply resort to *camera* trix, and the deed is did," he wrote to a friend.

The master mystifier with the great Charlie Chaplin

By then Houdini had veered onto a new career path. The man who had once advertised "I can make you a full-fledged medium!" began a crusade against spirit mediums. The common misconception is that Houdini's anger began to be directed against spirit mediums after he had failed to make contact with his dear departed mother in numerous sessions with bogus mediums. The reality is that the seeds of Houdini's campaign go back as early as 1906, when, in his first book, *The Right Way to Do Wrong,* a moralistic exposé of the cunning ways criminals exploit victims, he devoted a chapter to exposing

THE CELL-PHONE PSYCHIC

oudini often amazed his friends by leaving his living room, locking himself up on the third floor, then returning and guessing the object his friends were concentrating on. He accomplished this feat of thought transference with a primitive bugging device that relayed their conversations to his hiding place.

You can achieve the same results with your own cell phone, as long as it has a silent mode, an auto-answer function, and an earpiece with a microphone. Say you're at a big table at a restaurant eating with a bunch of your friends. Excuse yourself to go the bathroom, and when you come back you'll have heard everything that was said while you were gone. The way you do this is to leave your cell phone on the table with the earpiece connected. Set your phone to ring silently and to answer on ring. Don't forget to disable the vibrating ringer if you have one. Then, when you get to the bathroom area, look for a pay phone and call your cell phone. You'll be connected, no one will know the phone even rang, and the microphone will broadcast whatever anyone at the table is saying.

phony faith healers, spirit mediums, clairvoyants, and astrologers.

In fact, one could argue that one of the reasons Houdini lashed out against spirit mediums was that he saw them as competition. The magician's files contained many stories of mediums who used Houdini-like escapes, including one who in 1910 was doing a variation of Houdini's trunk substitution and using it as evidence of his supernatural abilities.

Many magicians had exposed spiritualist effects, both onstage and in court proceedings against mediums, but while on tour Houdini would don disguises and, with his own army of investigators, infiltrate séances of local mediums. Then, before his packed houses, which included the mediums and their supporters, Houdini would shine the spotlights on the phony mediums and level his accusations. Near riots would often break out. Of course, it all received tremendous newspaper coverage.

These medium exposures gave Houdini even more legitimacy. In 1924 he published his best book, *A Magician Among the Spirits*, a thoroughly researched, entertaining exposé of spirit manifesters both contemporary and historical. He served on a prestigious *Scientific American* committee that offered reward money to anyone who could prove he or she had legitimate supernatural powers. Although pretenders to the prize often fooled the other committee members, mostly academics, Houdini would always uncover the deceptions. "It takes a flimflammer to catch a flimflammer," he told the *Los Angeles Times* in 1924.

In 1926 he testified before Congress, spearheading proposed legislation against phony mediums. ("We have prohibition of alcohol, we have prohibition of drugs, but we have no law to prevent these human leeches from sucking every bit of reason and common sense from their victims," he wrote in *A Magician Among the Spirits*.) At the hearings Houdini was denounced by the other side as an atheist, a madman, a secret agent of the Elders of Zion sent to undermine the Christian faith, *and* a tool of the Pope.

By 1926 Houdini was fifty-two. A hit on the lecture circuit, he was planning to do a similar exposé of fraudulent gamblers and cardsharps. He was also intent on establishing "the first college of magic in the world," whose tentative curriculum including courses on magic history and philosophy, advertising, and showmanship. He began work on a book about superstition that included a history of witchcraft and astrology. He even planned to take courses in English at Columbia.

First, though, he still had some magic left in him. Since 1925 he had been fulfilling his lifelong ambition, touring with his own two-and-a-half-hour, full-fledged magic show, complete with big illusions and a bevy of sexy female assistants (under the watchful eye of Bess). He was getting rave reviews for the show, which featured magic, escapes, and exposés of spirit mediums. Then in Albany in October 1926, Houdini broke his ankle while he was being lifted into the Water Torture Cell. As usual, he shrugged off the injury and continued the tour.

In Montreal, despite his pain he lectured at McGill University. The next day two students visited him in his dressing room. One of them, Samuel Smilovitz, began drawing Houdini's portrait as the magician went through his mail and chatted about the movie business. Another student named Whitehead entered the room. The talk turned to physical strength. "Is it true, Mr. Houdini, that you can resist the hardest blows struck to the abdomen?" Whitehead inquired.

Houdini ignored the question, but Whitehead was persistent. "Would you mind if I delivered a few blows to your abdomen, Mr. Houdini?"

It was the last challenge Houdini would accept. Without giving Houdini time to tense his muscles or even get up off the couch, Whitehead delivered at least four "terribly forceful, deliberate, well-directed" blows to Houdini's lower stomach, according to Smilovitz. Then Houdini held up his hand and mumbled, "That will do." Smilovitz was allowed to finish his portrait. When the three boys began to leave, Houdini thanked Smilovitz for the sketch and told him, "You made me look a little tired in this picture. The truth is, I don't feel so well."

By the next day Houdini was in such pain that he had to lie down during the intermissions of his show. After the show he couldn't even dress himself. A wire was sent for a doctor to meet the troupe in Detroit, the next stop. Houdini was examined backstage. His temperature was 102 degrees. The physician suspected acute appendicitis and suggested that the magician be immediately hospitalized, but Houdini refused. He knew the house was sold out. "They're here to see me," he told the worried doctor. "I won't disappoint them."

To the stirring strains of "Pomp and Circumstance," Harry Houdini limped onto the stage. "We have had a thousand-mile journey and we are tired," he said. Then he began the show, but he could barely get through the simplest effects. When he magically

Houdini surrounded by spectators at an outdoor stunt in Sioux City

produced silk streamers, he was too weak to unfurl a whole streamer, and an assistant had to help him.

At the intermission he collapsed in his dressing room, his temperature having soared to 104 degrees, but still he persevered and somehow finished the show. Racked with pain, he made an impressive departure from his last stage. He bowed, said good-bye to the audience, then walked backward, bowing at each step, willing himself not to collapse.

Once the curtain closed he did collapse, but he still refused medical attention. He rested at the hotel until Bess's hysterical fit sent him to the hospital a few hours later. Even on entering the hospital early that Monday morning, Houdini refused to acknowledge the severity of his condition, joking with two burly attendants that he was still strong enough to lick 'em both. That afternoon his ruptured appendix was removed. Unfortunately, peritonitis had set in. Somehow, quite incredibly, Houdini had fought the toxins raging through his system. (For a long time people thought the ruptured appendix was a direct result of Whitehead's blows, but leading gastroenterologists doubt that a blow to the area can cause an appendix to rupture. Houdini probably was already suffering from appendicitis when he took Whitehead's challenge. The blows to his stomach merely gave him a rationale to ignore the pain until it was too late.)

Houdini was a model patient. He complimented the doctors, telling them that they were doing something worthwhile for mankind. He thanked every attendant who wiped his brow or gave him a sip of water. He joked with his visiting siblings, but on Friday he had a relapse and a second operation was performed. Sunday morning, October 31, Halloween, Houdini was barely strong enough to whisper to Hardeen: "I'm tired of fighting. I guess this thing is going to get me." Later that afternoon Bess was hugging him. He opened his eyes, saw her tears, and then his eyes slowly closed. Ehrich Weiss was dead.

Houdini, of course, lived on. He was probably the first dead person to be represented by a press agent when Bess hired a flack to keep his legend alive. She hawked his story around Hollywood for years, and in 1953 a wildly inaccurate movie of his life was released with Tony Curtis playing Harry. Houdini never receded into the mists of history. His life has been dissected by a score of biographers, most blinded by their preconceptions. One writer argued that he was impotent, another saw his rope and chain escapes as part of

a sadomasochistic drive. One psychiatrist even argued that Houdini loved to visit graveyards because when he was standing before the horizontal inhabitants of the graves, he felt most erect and alive.

All these theories pale in the face of the man. No other magician ever came close to elevating the art to the heights he did. There was only one Houdini—one person who could summon up the requisite skill and dedication and nerve and will and charisma to enchant and inspire millions of people throughout the world. For his entire life he lived and breathed magic—whether he was escaping from handcuffs twenty times a day in a seedy dime museum or planning a university devoted to the art from the plush confines of his Manhattan brownstone. Even at death's door, Houdini refused to disappoint his audience. He never did.

Houdini in Nice, France, in his later years

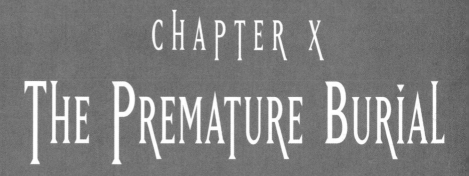

To be buried alive is, beyond question, the most terrific of . . . extremes. . . . We know of nothing so agonizing upon Earth.

—Edgar Allan Poe

The Premature Burial

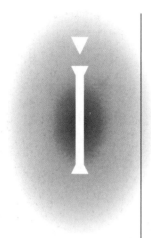

Note to the reader: To fully appreciate this chapter, I suggest that you read it while confined in a very small space, or, if that's not possible, lie perfectly still in your bed. Now imagine 168 hours of this.

n the summer of 1915, a thirty-nine-year-old black woman from South Carolina named Essie Dunbar suffered a severe epilepsy attack and was declared dead. The next morning she was buried after being eulogized by no fewer than three preachers. Despite the lengthy service, Essie's sister, who lived in a neighboring town, didn't arrive until after the burial was complete. Because she was distraught over not having seen her sister before the interment, the ministers agreed to dig up the coffin and allow the sister to pay her final respects face-to-face. When they opened the lid, Essie sat up and smiled at her sister.

All hell broke loose. The three shocked ministers fell backward into the grave, and one of them suffered broken ribs as the other two scrambled over him to safety. Believing they had seen a ghost, the mourners, including Essie's tardy sister, fled in horror, only to be pursued by Essie. When it was established that she was still alive, Essie became a local celebrity, lauded by some and shunned by others, who were convinced that she was a zombie. She finally died for real in 1955.

Being buried alive has always been one of humanity's most primal fears. In the mid-nineteenth century, when Poe wrote his "Premature Burial," it was a fear shared by millions. Folklore was replete with stories of people who had been mistakenly buried while still alive, and when their remains were disinterred there seemed to be signs of violent struggle to escape the coffin. There was even "evidence" that some of the unlucky victims had chewed off their hands in their horror. Although most, if not all, of these stories were apocryphal and there were explanations for all the strange effects that were happening in the coffins (rats chewing the hands, bodies bloating in the putrefaction process, et cetera), people's fears were real enough that some creative inventors began pro-

ducing security coffins that featured trapdoors, ladders, shovels, bells and whistles, and even refrigerators stocked with food, in case the interred regained consciousness. Some of their inventors gave well-attended public demonstrations of their coffins.

Being buried alive voluntarily transcends the mere promotion of security coffins. There's a rich tradition of self-interments in magic history. In fact, I initially got the idea to do a buried alive stunt after Bill Kalush and I perused a few of his books that chronicled the feats of the Indian fakirs known as the *jadoo-wallahs*. The *jadoo-wallahs* were renowned for talents as diverse as snake charming, human pincushion effects, relaxing on beds of nails, and fire walking, but the feat that fascinated me the most was their practice of being buried alive.

One of the earliest documented accounts of voluntary live burial occurred in Amritsar, India, in the middle of the seventeenth century. While digging a drainage ditch on the outskirts of town, laborers were amazed to discover a shallow tomb that contained a remarkably well-preserved body of a young, bearded sadhu, or Indian holy man. He was wearing an orange shawl and sat in the customary cross-legged yogic burial position. They were about to leave him at rest, but there was something eerie about his appearance so the workers carried his body to the surface. Then, as soon as he was swathed in the sun's rays, the sadhu began to stir. Within minutes he had wobbled to his feet while the workers prostrated themselves at this great miracle.

A month later this guru was known all over India. His name was Ramaswamy, and he claimed that he had been buried in that tomb for a hundred years. When questioned by leading scholars of the day, Ramaswamy provided accurate details of events of the century before. With this accreditation, Rama-

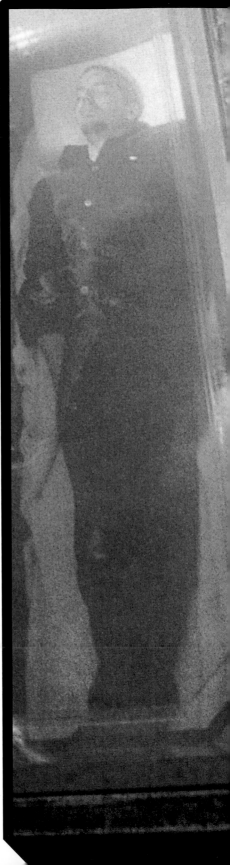

swamy gained a large following that supported him in style for the rest of his life.

Ramaswamy was rivaled in popularity by another guru who buried himself alive many times in the 1800s. Haridas, who came from the same region as Ramaswamy, went underground for up to four months at a time. In 1835 the *Calcutta Medical Journal* carried a complete account of one of these burials. Before the burial a team of doctors examined Haridas. They discovered that the sadhu had cut away the muscles under his tongue so that he could voluntarily move his tongue back to seal his throat. Haridas's preparations for the burial included natural laxatives, hot water baths, and a diet of yogurt and milk.

On the day of the burial, to expel any foreign matter left in his stomach, Haridas swallowed a thirty-yard-long piece of linen and then extracted it. He sat in the cross-legged position, sealed his ears and nostrils with wax, swallowed his tongue, folded his arms, and went into a trance. The doctors' examination showed no pulse. Haridas's body was then wrapped in linen and placed in a large chest, which was padlocked and sealed with the maharaja's personal seal. The chest was buried in a garden, a wall was built around it, and guards were stationed twenty-four hours a day.

Forty days later the doctors and officials reconvened at the site. The chest was dug up and unlocked, and Haridas appeared cold and stiff. The doctors pulled his tongue back, unplugged his nose and ears, and gave him mouth-to-mouth resuscitation. Within an hour

the yogi was back to normal. He repeated this feat in many other cities, garnering a large following, who provided him with all his material wants, including the virginity of several of his devotees. A scandal ensued, and the government wound up banishing Haridas to the mountains. He was never heard from again.

Many fakirs continued this tradition. It reached its ultimate exploitation in the 1920s, when an Egyptian named Rahman Bey toured the world vaudeville circuits doing a living burial routine. He would lie down in a coffin, go into a "self-hypnotic trance" that would presumably stop his pulse, and be buried alive from a few minutes to a few days, depending on how closely his performance was audited. He was a sensation in the Middle East and Europe, but when he came to America the press was skeptical.

To quiet the naysayers, Bey gave a public demonstration in New York City in 1926. He got into an air- and watertight coffin and was lowered into the Hudson River. He planned to stay submerged for an hour, but after only four minutes, as the coffin was being lowered into the water, the emergency alarm went off. By the time the workmen pulled the coffin up and unsealed it, Bey could boast that, thanks to his powers of self-hypnosis, he had managed to survive without air for almost twenty minutes. What he didn't publicize was that a standard coffin would provide enough air for a person to survive for up to twenty-five minutes.

Bey's display of obvious charlatanism enraged Harry Houdini, who pounced on it as another chance to expose fakirism. Houdini issued a challenge to Bey. He would "guarantee to remain in any coffin that the fakir [Bey] does for the same length of time that he does, without going into any cataleptic trance." Bey responded by duplicating his underwater feat at a New York City swimming school. This time he was soldered into a casket poolside, where he remained for thirty-six minutes. Then the casket was lowered into the pool, and he stayed underwater for another twenty-four minutes. Now Houdini had to stay underwater for an hour.

Houdini didn't take this challenge lightly. He began serious training and lost thirteen pounds. With a large assemblage of the press present, he entered his own custom-made watertight casket and was lowered to the bottom of the pool of the Hotel Shelton in New York City. He carefully rationed his breath and managed to stay buried underwater for an hour and a half, smashing Bey's record. When he was brought up, his pulse was 142, and he was ashen-faced and groggy. Hours later he was still listless and wobbly and had a weird metallic taste in his mouth. Houdini never repeated this feat.

Houdini had not been as successful when he was buried alive in the ground eleven years earlier. According to his own account, in 1915 he had made a bet that he could be manacled and buried six feet belowground and get back "to the land of living" without any assistance. Houdini's only condition was that the burials be graded, first escaping from one foot under, then two, slowly working his way to six feet deep. Houdini and his party left Los Angeles at dawn and drove to Santa Ana, where he knew the soil was sandy and would allow some oxygen to penetrate it. He breezed through the shallow burials, but he had some difficulty with the four- and five-foot plantings. Then, when he attempted to escape from a six-foot grave, he got the scare of his life:

> The knowledge that I was six feet under sod—the legal requirement for corpses—gave me the first thrill of horror I had ever experienced in my career as a journeyman daredevil. The momentary scare—the irretrievable mistake of all daredevils—nearly cost me my life, for it caused me to waste a fraction of breath when every fraction was needed to pull through. I had kept the sand loose about my body so that I could work dexterously. I did. But as I clawed and kneed the earth my strength began to fail. Then I made another mistake. I yelled. Or, at least, I attempted to, and the last remnants of my self-possession left me. Then instinct stepped in to the rescue. With my last reserve I fought through, more sand than air entering my nostrils. The sunlight came like a blinding blessing, and my friends about the grave said that, chalky pale and wild-eyed as I was, I presented a perfect imitation of a dead man rising. The next time I'm buried it will not be alive—if I can help it.

Seven days and seven nights of complete deprivation

Although Houdini would never try it again, by the 1950s burying oneself alive was common practice in India. The sincere holy men who attempted this feat without resorting to trickery invariably wound up suffocated and dead. Their numbers were so large that in 1955 the Indian government formally outlawed living burials, but many fakirs disregarded the law and continued to build large followings by faking their burials. A young American journalist named John Keel traveled to Banaras, India, in the 1950s and exposed these fake burials (as well as other practices of the fakirs) in a remarkable memoir entitled *Jadoo*.

Keel suggested that the fakirs used at least two tricks. The simplest was to employ a coffin with a fake bottom. The initial ceremony would take place in a temple. The fakir, surrounded by his followers, would enter the coffin. The lid would be impressively nailed shut, then the coffin would be hoisted up and carried out to the burial grounds. But during the ceremony the fakir would change into a robe and turban identical to those of his followers, who would have obscured the coffin from view. Escaping from the false bottom, the disguised fakir would blend in with the followers and help carry the coffin to the burial site. The coffin would be buried, and the fakir would go into hiding for a year. When the coffin was dug up, the process would be reversed: the fakir would slip back in and emerge unscathed in the temple.

Another, more elaborate ruse involved a tunnel dug from the burial site to a distant point, usually surrounded by trees. Again the coffin would have been fixed so that an escape could be made through a sliding panel. This time the fakir would actually be in the coffin when it was lowered into the ground, but he would slip out through the panel, burrow along the pre-dug tunnel, and make his escape far from the burial site. Just before disinterment he would reverse the process and climb back into the coffin.

Chinese prisoners being buried alive against their will, never to return, by their Japanese captors. Nanjing, 1938.

Some fakirs actually did get buried. They'd lie on rough boards and let the dirt be shoveled right on top of them. Keel even enticed a fakir named Govindaswamy to teach him how to be buried alive. Govindaswamy gave Keel some practical tips: say special holy words, make your mind go blank, hold your breath, and drink no water for several hours before the burial. He showed Keel a method that utilized a small stone to stop his pulse. The fakir also suggested that Keel put his hands over his ears to keep the bugs out and breathe only through his nose.

After Keel made an ample donation in U.S. currency, Govindaswamy arranged for both of them to be buried alive. Two graves were dug, side by side. Keel and the fakir lay down on planks, and then another plank was lowered over them. Keel was given a string that he was to pull to signal to the aboveground attendants that he wanted to be dug out. Then the dirt was filled in. The graves were three and a half feet deep, and the soil was loose and porous enough to admit air, so Keel had no trouble breathing. After what seemed to be an eternity, he had had enough and pulled the string. But it was stuck in the dirt. He yanked at the string for what seemed like several minutes and was about to use up his precious air in a last desperate shout for freedom when he heard the sound of shovels above him. Moments later he was back in the cool night air. He had been buried alive for thirty minutes. Govindaswamy was duly impressed when *he* was dug up—thirty minutes later.

Outside India very few people have attempted to be buried alive. In the early 1900s an entertainer named Kar-Mi claimed to have been buried alive for thirty-two days in India but, according to his handbill, the "federal authorities" prohibited him from re-

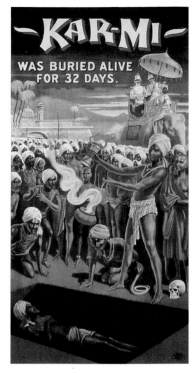

(top left) *Rahman Bey's underwater burial in New York's Hudson River, a stunt that inspired Houdini's Shelton Pool challenge.*
(top right) *A poster for Kar-Mi, an early twentieth-century performer who replicated Indian fakir effects*

creating his "sleep of Death" during his performances in Madison Square Garden in New York City. His audiences had to be content to watch him identify objects while blindfolded and marvel at his "actual swallowing and exploding (while still in the body) of a fully charged army musket barrel, as well as other performances that seem utterly at variance with any of the known laws of nature."

A few years earlier a pain resister named Tommy Minnock was "hypnotized" by the French physician Charcot in Antwerp and then buried alive for four days. Doctors deduced that the hypnosis had worked when they were unable to find a pulse and when Minnock showed no sign of pain when hot irons were pressed to his body. Minnock later revealed that he was far from hypnotized—in fact, when the doctors weren't examining him, his nurse, a confederate, pulled some rubber bottles filled with liquid refreshments from under her dress and slipped them to the seemingly somnolent pain resister.

A few years later Minnock was hired to repeat the Charcot burial test in Connecticut. Minnock was furious when Santinelli, the "hypnotist" with whom he was working this time, agreed to an aboveground burial in which Minnock could be continually monitored by the doctors and their own nurse. Minnock recounted his ordeal a few years later to Houdini: "I was in the coffin in agony for ninety-six hours, without food or drink, and could hear Santinelli with a good full stomach putting up a dandy bluff to the doctors." Minnock proceeded to expose the "hypnotic demonstrations" of both Charcot and Santinelli (after the newspaper the *New York*

(below) *The inexplicable black cross hovering over the casket. This is a photo captured from an onlooker's home video.*

World paid him a nice fee); then he vanished from the limelight.

Recently there have been attempts to duplicate Houdini's buried-alive trials, with disastrous results. In 1990 a performer died when his coffin collapsed under the weight of the earth. Two years later, an escapologist was handcuffed, locked inside a Plexiglas coffin, and buried under seven tons of cement. The coffin collapsed, and it took rescuers, using a backhoe, twenty-two minutes to pull him out. Fortunately, he survived.

In 1998 I was living in a six-foot-by-five-foot room off the kitchen of Bill Kalush's apartment in midtown Manhattan. Although I had enough money to have a place of my own, I loved that little room, which was stuffed with all my possessions and the spillover of Kalush's magic library. One day Kalush came in with an old book about the Indian fakirs. He suggested that we (or, to be more accurate, I) duplicate their stunt by being buried alive for a month in Central Park in New York City. Kalush figured that, like the fakirs, I could escape and go back in a month later.

I wanted to do it for real, for a week. Then we started arguing. The reason Kalush and I get along so well is that we argue about everything, and during that process the ideas get refined and stronger. Kalush, always the purist, wanted me to be buried under dirt. He figured that a few of my hard-core fans would come to check out my burial. My agent liked the idea and thought he could get a mention in the *New York Post.*

I immediately realized that, if I was going to be buried, it shouldn't be under dirt, because no one would believe that I was re-

(top) *A female spectator puts her hand in the water above the casket to make sure it is real.*
(below) *It was nice to have the support of the people of New York.*

ally down there. So we started playing with the idea of putting a hole above my head so people could see me. Then I realized that by combining the underground burial with the underwater burial, we'd have the perfect solution. After about a week of fighting over that, we finally agreed. I'd be buried six feet under the ground in a clear Plexiglas coffin, which would have a huge tank filled with water on top of it. My friend Uri Geller even suggested that I put sharks and octopi in the water.

When we approached people for financial support, nobody wanted to come near us. Eventually Jimmy Nederlander, the famed New York theater producer, agreed to put up the money, and then I called Donald Trump, who was happy to provide us with the burial site, which happened to be on the grounds of Trump Place, his new apartment complex on the west side of Manhattan. Nederlander called a visionary builder named Tom Bramlett, who worked out of Las Vegas. Bramlett was at first concerned that it would be too dangerous to be buried under the massive weight of that water. But after some engineering that would ensure my safety, he called back and said it could be done. A few months later he had designed an elaborate burial site.

I would be put to rest in a clear coffin that had a thin mat and an ample supply of air. The coffin would be lit, so I'd be visible to any spectators, day or night. Tom engineered a huge drainage system so any heavy rains wouldn't flood me out. The acrylic casing for the 4,500 pounds of water that would be on top of me would be an inch and a quarter thick, and a heavy steel frame would bolster that tank. The lid on the coffin would also be an inch and a quarter thick—a .44 Magnum couldn't penetrate that much acrylic.

While all this was going on, I had to be sure that I could stay confined for a week with just inches of wiggle room, so I bought a metal practice coffin. Kalush and I purchased it from the same family who made the casket Houdini used for the Bey challenge. We set the coffin up in the living room, and I began practicing. At first, when we were still thinking of doing my version of the Shelton pool stunt, I'd climb into the coffin and Kalush would turn the key, rendering it airtight. After forty-five minutes or so, I'd tap on the lid and he would unlock it.

After we had decided that I'd stay underground for a week, I began to spend longer amounts of time in the coffin. I'd grab my cell phone so I could conduct business and climb in, leaving the lid cracked a little so I could get air and light. I'd hang out like that for days, taking occasional bathroom breaks. I always fasted, so I was used to not eating. Not using a phone was another story.

When I had worked up to staying in the coffin for four days, I stopped practicing. Why torture myself any further? I knew that if I could do four, I could do seven. Little did I really know. Even though I was confident I could stay in the coffin for seven days, every doctor I consulted before the burial warned me not to go ahead with it. It was hard even to get doctors to talk with me about this, they were so afraid of malpractice suits, but the ones who would talk warned me that if I didn't breathe right in the coffin, I could get pneumonia and my heart could stop. They were also concerned about muscle atrophy and dehydration. To make sure that I would be okay, we hired a nurse who taught me hand signals to let her know if I was in any kind of distress.

I wasn't nervous at all before the burial. But, looking back, I can see that I sure was exhibiting all the side effects of anxiety. For a week before the event, I drank only juices and walked around feeling really spacey. The weekend before the burial, I couldn't read and didn't feel like talking to anyone; all I could do was stay holed up in the apartment and watch movies. My subconscious anxiety wasn't helped by Kalush, who, on the morning of the burial, told me that I didn't have to go through with it; he'd still be my friend if I backed out. There was no way in the world I'd do that, but I'm sure his concern increased my own hypochondria. I kept reminding myself to breathe deeply, so I wouldn't wind up with pneumonia.

I had originally planned to be buried on Good Friday, and I was going to spend my birthday, which fell that year on Easter Sunday, underground, but we delayed it until the religious holiday was over.

NEW YORK NOW

CLASS ACT Graduation-style advice inspires hit song. MUSIC Page 42

DAVID HALBERSTAM THE CHILDREN

BETWEEN COVERS Four good reads perfect for waiting out April showers. BOOKS Page 42

APRIL 5, 1999 • ARTS • ENTERTAINMENT • LIFESTYLE

The Next Houdini

GRIN & BERRA: Yogi gets a look at himself.

MELAYNE SEIDMAN

Take Me Out to The Yogi Berra Museum

The beloved Yank gets his due with a Jersey shrine to his career

Page 41

Magician David Blaine is being buried alive today on the West Side

Page 40

New York Daily News

Time Out New York

The obsessive guide to impulsive entertainment
April 1-8, 1999 Issue No. 184 $2.50

Interviews
Robert Altman
Derek Jeter
Nas

Eye-popping eyewear

Open your own restaurant

This is Hell Week!
Magician
David Blaine
gets buried alive for seven days

Plus
The mysterious magic tour

That Monday we got to the site early. I was amazed how many media people had shown up. Donald Trump made a short speech, and I waved to the crowd. "I'll see you guys in a week," I said. Then I was buried alive.

Most people believed that to be buried alive you'd have to put yourself into a deep trance state, but I didn't think that was true. I thought I'd just go into the box, shut my eyes, and lie there. I had practiced in the living room, and I never once felt claustrophobic. I had a tube so I could pee and a supply of water if I got thirsty. I expected the burial to be only slightly harder than lying on my living room couch.

I couldn't have been more wrong. Once I felt that *whoosh,* and I was sealed in the coffin and that huge container of water was placed on top of me, I realized all that training in the living room didn't help me one iota. I immediately panicked. There was no way out. On top of that, when they lowered the water tank on top of me, it bumped against the sides of the enclosure. After a few minutes, I was convinced that something had gone wrong and my air supply wasn't working. The first sixty minutes were sheer hell, with me worrying that I was depleting what little air I had. After an hour I realized that my air supply was fine. Then I only had to worry about what else could go wrong for seven days.

All these thoughts kept racing through my head, but I made a conscious effort to calm down. I tried to sleep, but it wasn't possible to get any deep sleep. Being able to see out was nice, but the water refracted the light and the sun was beating down on me during the day, so it was hard to make out distinct images. Everything, especially the steady stream of people who looked down at me like I was an animal in the zoo, looked surreal.

One minute didn't go by that whole week without lightbulbs flashing in my face from people taking my picture. To make matters worse, a newsperson had broadcast that there was a chance I really wasn't in the coffin and my image was just a hologram, so then people aimed those small, incredibly bright laser beam pointers into my face to make sure I was real. It was tough.

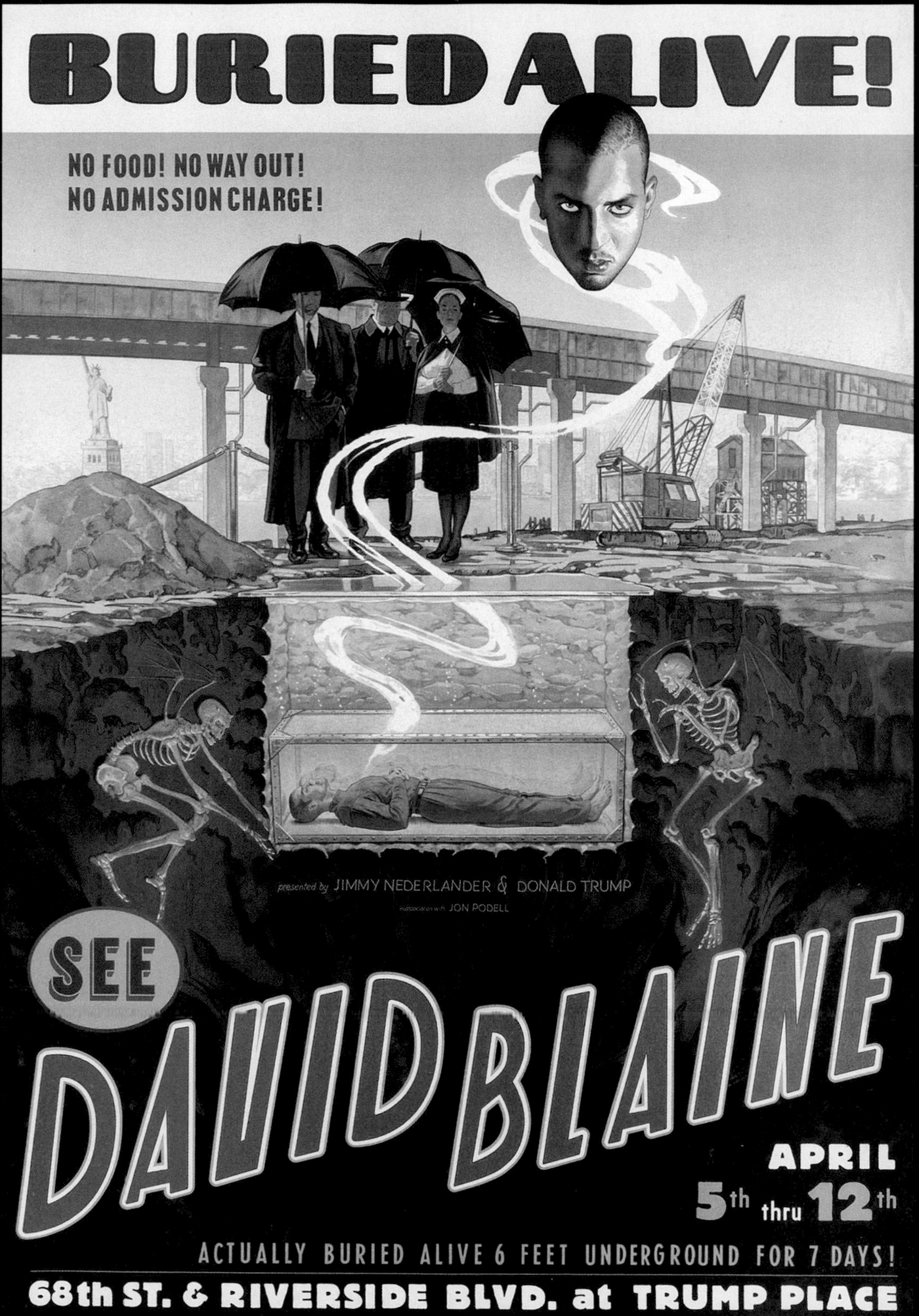
BURIED ALIVE!
NO FOOD! NO WAY OUT!
NO ADMISSION CHARGE!
presented by JIMMY NEDERLANDER & DONALD TRUMP
JON PODELL
SEE
DAVID BLAINE
APRIL
5th thru 12th
ACTUALLY BURIED ALIVE 6 FEET UNDERGROUND FOR 7 DAYS!
68th ST. & RIVERSIDE BLVD. at TRUMP PLACE

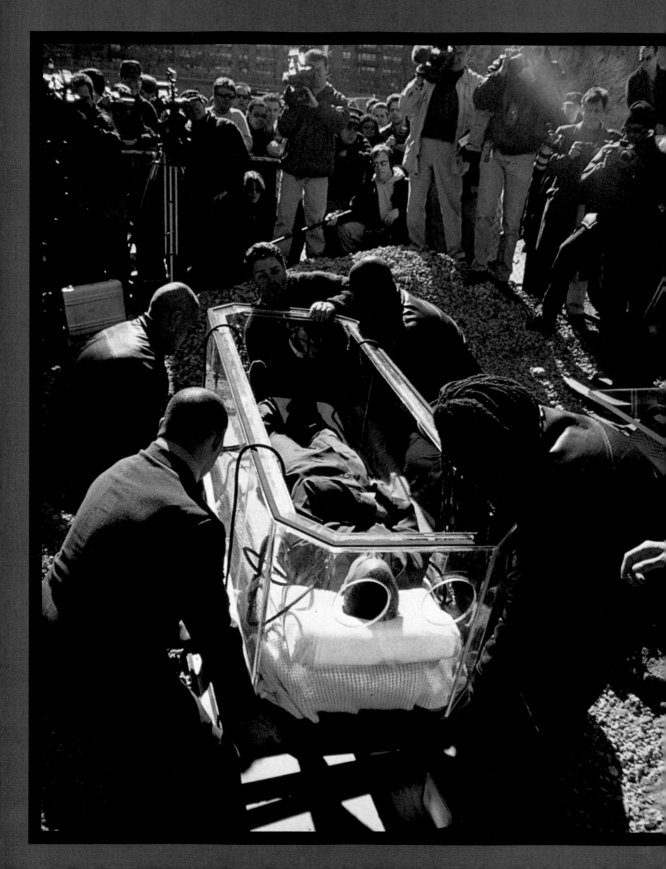

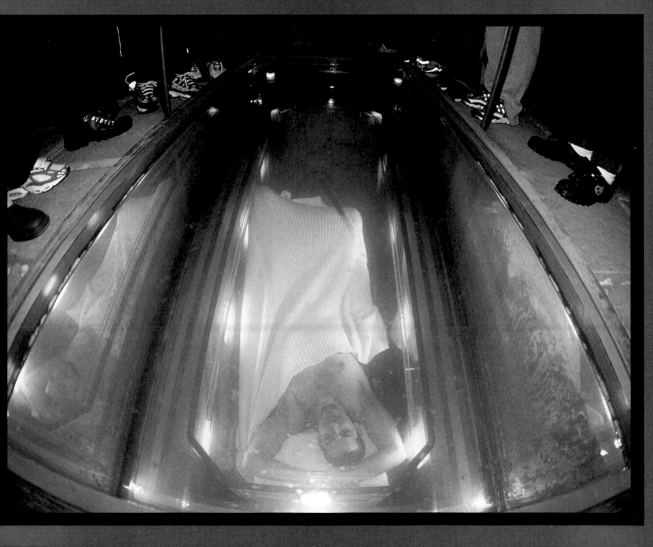

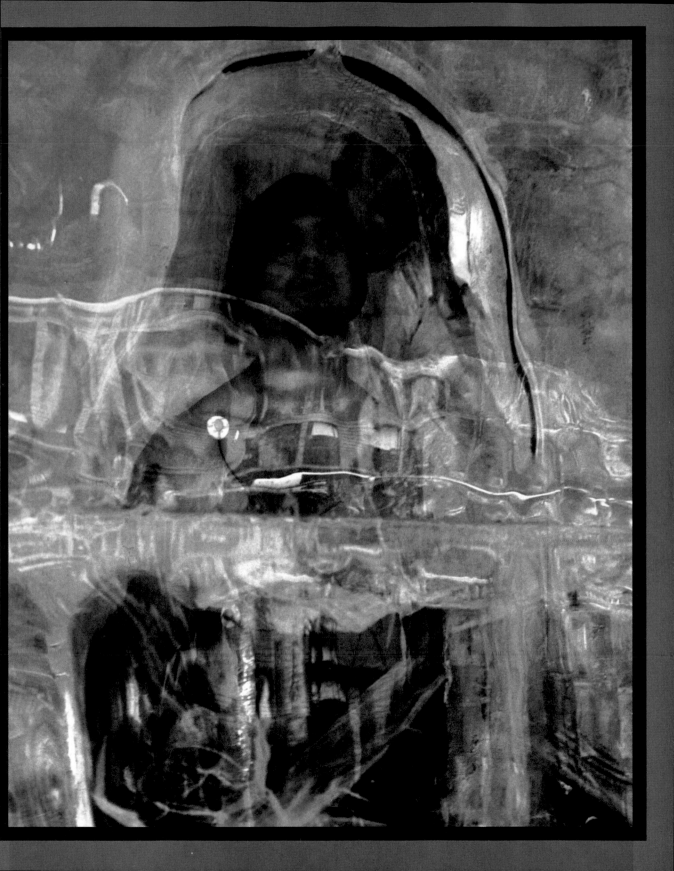

POLICE LINE DO NOT CROSS
POLICE DEPT.

DAVID
BLAINE'S
WILL HE LIVE?
MAY 21-22, 2002
WITNESS THE EVENT
IN PERSON AT
BRYANT PARK
42ND STREET
BETWEEN
5TH & 6TH AVE.
NEW YORK CITY
BROADCAST LIVE ON ABC AT 10:00 PM ON MAY 22ND
VERTIGO

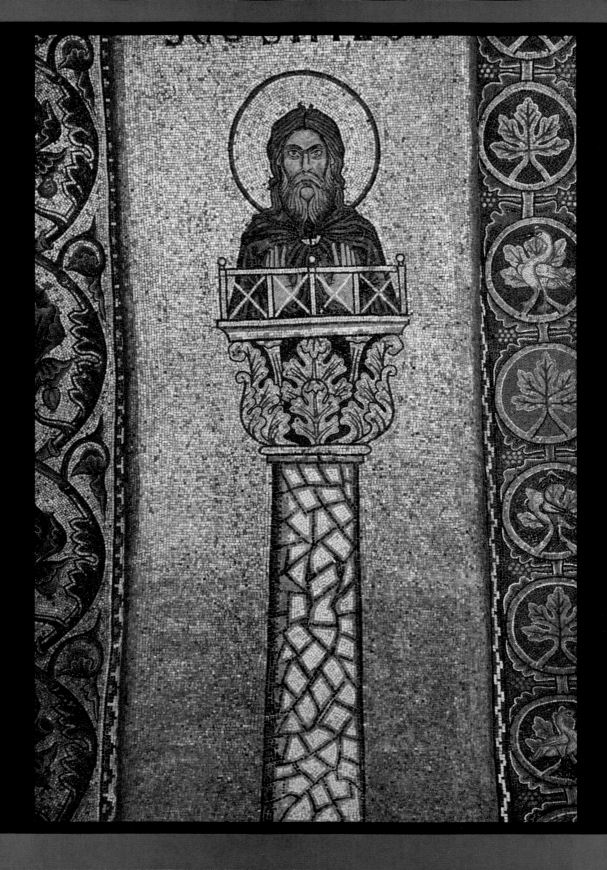

The first highlight for me came when I got over my inhibitions and was able to pee while waving to the people peering in at me. For most of the first day, I had been a little gun-shy and couldn't urinate. Finally, I closed my eyes and pretended I was standing in front of a toilet, and it worked. When I was finally able to pee and wave at the same time, I was ecstatic. I wasn't so ecstatic about the catheter the nurse had outfitted for me. Bramlett had engineered a drainage hole in the bottom of the casket so I could just roll over and whatever I voided would drain right out. When I got in the coffin I had a catheter hooked up, but the tube that led to the drainage hole wasn't fed right, so I wound up peeing all over the mat most of the time I was underground. Luckily for me, I was so paranoid about running out of the water supply in the coffin that I drank only about two gallons of water the whole week.

Funkiness aside, the burial was a success way beyond our

Kalush (right) *helps me up after a week underground. When I came out I saw the world differently. I was also twenty-four pounds lighter.*

wildest expectations. By my third day in the coffin, ropes had to be set up and lines formed to accommodate all the people who wanted to pass by and wave at me. At points the lines stretched for twelve blocks. It's estimated that almost half a million New Yorkers came to visit. The media covered the whole event, giving live updates from the coffin. Weathermen did their forecasts from the site. We got coverage all over the world, including front-page coverage in all the newspapers in India. They were really interested in an American who was replicating the feats of their fakirs.

Houdini's octogenarian niece stopped by and told the press that he would have been "thrilled that this boy was doing this because he would know the stamina it takes." Michael Jackson showed up in disguise. I was really touched by the working cops and firemen who would make daily pilgrimages to make sure that I was all right. When it rained people came and told Kalush they felt guilty that they were home, safe and warm, while I was lying in the ground. One woman came every day and stayed for hours on end. She finally explained to Kalush that she had always been claustrophobic and by watching me was finally able to get over her fear.

After the third day I began to get extremely uncomfortable and suffered aches and pains in places I didn't even know existed. I couldn't really sleep, so I began to hallucinate. My hands looked like spiders. I had horrible visions of concentration camps and prisoner of war compounds. By now the hours really seemed to drag. Thank God my brother, who was there the whole time, held up a sign so I could see how much time I had left. He was a real champ.

Strange things happened too. After the event was over, I got a video from a woman who lived in the building directly in front of my burial site. She had kept her video camera rolling the whole time, and the strangest thing happened right before dawn on the second day. Her video shows that a perfectly formed black cross hovered above my coffin for over an hour that morning. We took the video to ABC, and their technicians determined that it wasn't doctored in any way, but they had no explanation for the cross. Even stranger, you couldn't see the cross from the ground. Kalush, who was there the entire week, didn't see it. The technicians didn't see it. The nurse didn't see it.

The most unbelievable thing happened right before I was about to be released. The only thing I brought into the coffin with me was a picture of my mom. In many ways I was enduring a week buried underground as a tribute to her, since she had endured so much aboveground before she died, without ever complaining. That morning it had been raining and I said to myself, "Mom, if you're here, show me a sign. Make the sun come out." Suddenly the clouds ripped open, the rain stopped, and the sun burst out. My eyes teared up.

When they lifted the lid of my glass coffin, I smelled that beautiful spring air, and I felt like I was being reborn. Then I saw that I was surrounded by a sea of smiling faces who all looked different. There were old Jewish Hasids standing next to Muslim cab-drivers who were next to black kids. Businessmen in designer suits stood beside heavily pierced street kids. Every conceivable social type was represented. I was a little weak, and I had lost twenty-four pounds (I hadn't eaten anything for six days *before* the burial either), but I had enough strength to take the microphone and salute the crowd: "I saw something truly incredible. . . . I saw every race, every age-group, and every religion gathered together smiling, and that made everything worth it."

I saw magic.

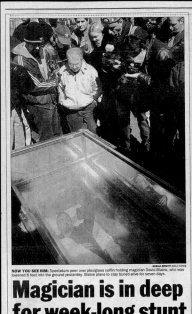

CHAPTER XI

FROZEN IN TIME²

*I submit to you
that if a man hasn't discovered
something he would die for,
he isn't fit to live.*

—Dr. Martin Luther King, Jr.

Frozen in Time[2]

I was sure I was dead. I didn't know where I was. I was surrounded by thousands of people who were all staring at me, but I couldn't communicate with any of them. I couldn't even feel anything. For a second I thought this was Purgatory and we were all waiting to be judged. Then this chilling feeling of déjà vu swept over me. I *had* been here before. Maybe this was just a bad dream. Strange, indecipherable thoughts shot through my brain. I kept hearing the Munchkin song from *The Wizard of Oz,* but the tempo was all speeded up.

Suddenly I recognized my then girlfriend Josie. She was standing in front of me. She looked up and smiled and I reached out to touch her, but there was this weird transparent wall between us. I touched it, and it was freezing. I wanted to talk to her real bad, but I couldn't get through that wall. Then I tasted something salty. It was tears, and I realized that they were flowing down my cheeks. My whole body started convulsing from the sobs. Suddenly Josie was sitting on top of the transparent wall, waving at me. I reached up to her, but she just vanished; then she was in front of me. I called out to her, but she just turned away. Now I was sure I was dead. That was the last thing I remembered.

"I don't like the way he looks. We should get him out now."

"He can't come out of the ice now, we have to break for commercial. Keep him in there."

"David, are you all right? You want out?"

"We're back live. Just minutes ago, David said, 'I want out. I want out now!' But it's a very large piece of ice—structurally they have to be very careful."

"Pull him out gently."

"He can't stand up on his own."

"Quick, get him a chair."

"He's out now. His legs are wobbly. He looks very disoriented. His clothes

are soaking wet. We have to remind you that for three days he's had no food, just water."

"Da-vid! Da-vid! Da-vid!"

"Get some blankets on him. Okay, give him the mike. He's going to make his statement."

"Josie. My mind. My mind. Something's wrong."

"He's totally incoherent. Ad-lib something."

"I think he's just mentally and emotionally frustrated. It's very difficult, folks. Understand, sleep deprivation for three days, standing in the ice on the street, no food. You can tell right now he's a little disoriented. They're gonna take him away."

"Put him right in the ambulance. I don't like the way he looks."

"He looks like he's going into shock."

"His doctor is standing by. Dr. Ruden, what's happened here?"

"After all this stress, he's been held together by spit and adrenaline. The adrenaline's now gone, and we have to make sure he doesn't go into shock now. We're going to take care of him."

"Da-vid! Da-vid! Da-vid!"

"Please back up. Please, back up."

"Get him in the ambulance. Where's Josie? Josie! Get Josie!"

"I want you to hold that ambulance. We have forty seconds till break."

"Look, he may be going into shock. Get away from that door. Close it up. Move those people away in front. Okay, go. Go. Go!"

There's an inherent problem with the challenges I take on. The latest one always has to top the last one. After I was buried alive for a week, I knew I had to do something that was far more dangerous and difficult. About two months after the burial, the idea came to me. I had been working on replicating Houdini's Chinese Water Torture Cell, and we had renderings made of me in the water tank. As I was looking at the drawings, it suddenly struck me that the tank resembled a giant block of ice.

I've always been fascinated by ice. There's something so powerful and beautiful and mysterious and dangerous about it. There is no sight more majestic than a tree with its branches cloaked in ice. When I was a kid, I'd pull down icicles and store them in my freezer. When a pond froze over, I'd run out and jump on it. There was always that fear, that risk that I'd fall right through the ice and die, but I was still drawn to the ice, running on it and jumping and trying to crack it.

My then girlfriend, Josie, keeps an eye on me in the ice.

I know a sculptor named Joe Ice, who carves the most unbeliev-able things out of ice. He'll create amazingly intricate portraits of people or even a full-sized person riding a motorcycle, all made of ice. For one party he carved a whole bar out of ice and set it up so that vodka would slide right down the ice into your mouth. Joe lives in Brooklyn, and he's always carving new huge ice sculptures, setting them up in his backyard and then dramatically backlighting them. People stop their cars, get out, and just stare at the ice.

I started imagining what it would look like if I were somehow encased in a big, beautiful block of ice. A few days later I got a call from Uri Geller, who told me that he had a dream in which I was frozen alive. That was the sign I needed. For my next challenge I was going to freeze myself in an enormous block of ice.

Unfortunately, there weren't too many precedents for this. Ma-gicians had certainly long used ice in their effects. Long Tack Sam often performed an effect that was a favorite of Chinese magicians. He would show the audience a bowl filled with water. Then he would dip out a handful of the water, pour it from hand to hand,

and mysteriously change the water in his hand into a small piece of ice, no matter how high the temperature in the room.

Max Malini was notorious for his own production of a large block of ice from under a hat. He did this effect standing at a bar or seated at a dinner table. He'd sit there for up to a half hour, then he'd typically ask a woman at the table if he could examine her hat. After complimenting the hat, he would start to hand it back to her, then change his mind and say, "Vait a meenut, I show you a leetle trick." He would borrow a half dollar, spin it on the table, and place the hat over the coin. He'd then ask one of the onlookers to guess whether the coin came up heads or tails ("Lady or Eagle?" he'd say). He'd do this two times, but when he lifted the hat on the third guess, the coin would have been replaced by a huge piece of ice.

Houdini, on the other hand, spent many years trying to devise an effect in which he would be encased in a huge block of ice that would be formed right before the audience's eyes, then escape from it. He planned to wear a diving suit and a helmet onstage. Then he would be lowered into a tank of water that had a see-through glass front. A chemical solution that would quickly induce freezing would be poured into the tank. Shortly after the water had turned to ice, entombing Houdini, the tank would be enclosed in a cabinet with cloth sides, and Houdini would free himself.

Putting this theoretical escape into practice proved impossible. For months Houdini tried to come up with a solution that would freeze the water quickly enough to make the escape palatable to the audience, but the technology at the time didn't allow it. During his experimentation Houdini caught a severe cold, and he abandoned the whole project.

Carnival performers did ice stunts, but they were very different from Houdini's planned effect. For one thing, they usually involved lying down on coffin-shaped blocks of ice. Even still, the daredevils, usually women, would lie on the ice for only an hour or at most two. They often wound up with pneumonia. The old carny ice stunt was revived by the "ordeal artist" Zhang Huan in 1998. He lay face down, naked, on an ice mattress at a performance art space, P.S. 1 in New York. Mr. Huan intended to lie there until the ice melted entirely, but after ten minutes his body temperature had plummeted and he jumped off the ice. "The fact that it wouldn't melt anymore had a kind of meaning in itself," he explained to the assembled press.

It's a scientific fact that humans were meant to live in tropical climates, although our species can make certain adaptations enabling us to live in a region like Siberia, where the temperature can sink as low as −90.4 degrees F. The bodies of the inhabitants of Siberian villages maintain a constant temperature in cold weather by restricting blood flow to the skin. These villagers also develop increased body hair, which traps a layer of air close to the skin that serves as insulation. They store greater reserves of fat, and their bodies become rounder and shorter to prevent heat loss.

Of course, all this adaptation means nothing when the earth experiences an ice age. In the 1920s a scientist named Milutin Milankovitch proved that Earth temporarily moves out of its orbit around the Sun approximately every hundred thousand years. This aberrant cycle can decrease the mean temperature by a degree and kick off an ice age. In the last 1.8 million years, our planet has experienced seventeen such ice ages.

What's scary is that it can take as little as 20 years for the transition from an interglacial period to an ice age. Ice ages have lingered for as long as 100,000 years. The interglacial periods, the times when human life can flourish on the planet, last a much shorter time. The shortest interglacial era was about 8,000 years. The longest lasted approximately 12,000 years. The interglacial warm period we are now in the midst of started about 11,800 years ago. What all this means is that we're long overdue for the next ice age and sometime in the near future, and it may be as soon as within

Early ice stunts: (top) Mr. Moro was frozen in a cake of ice for thirty minutes before being chopped out; (bottom) In 1946 Bobby Jones was sealed inside a five-hundred-pound block of ice, then flown from Atlantic City to New York City. He stayed in the ice for seven hours.

20 years, people in the Northern Hemisphere could wake up to a snowstorm that might last for the rest of their lives.

Forgetting even the ominous specter of an ice age, it's understandable that humans try to avoid prolonged contact with ice, because there is a real danger of developing hypothermia. The signs of hypothermia are dramatic. When your body temperature drops only a degree or two, shivering begins. At 96 degrees, you begin to feel chilly, your skin starts to get numb, and there's an immediate impairment in muscular performance. You can't coordinate your movements, and you fumble anything you try to hold. Between 95 and 93 degrees, your shivering becomes violent. You have difficulty speaking. Your coordination deteriorates rapidly. You begin to feel disoriented and apathetic. You feel numb all over, and your skin pales and is cold to the touch.

From 93 to 90 degrees, things get worse. You stumble and fall frequently. You lose control of your hands. Your brain feels sluggish, and you can hardly speak. You begin to develop amnesia. Between 89 and 86 degrees, although your shivering stops, you are unable to walk or even stand. Your whole body gets stiff. You become incoherent and irrational. When your temperature drops below 86 degrees, your muscles get rigid, your pupils dilate, your heartbeat slows down considerably, and your skin turns ice cold. When you hit 82 degrees, you become unconscious and, in most cases, you'll die from heart and respiratory failure.

I was well aware of these dangers, but I was still determined to go ahead with the ice endurance challenge. People are always asking me why I do these things to myself. I really don't have a concise answer to that question. Why did Houdini bury himself alive? He talked about overcoming fear, and that's an element in what I do. I know that when I push myself to the absolute limit, I feel more alive than ever.

People mention a death wish, but I don't think that's the case.

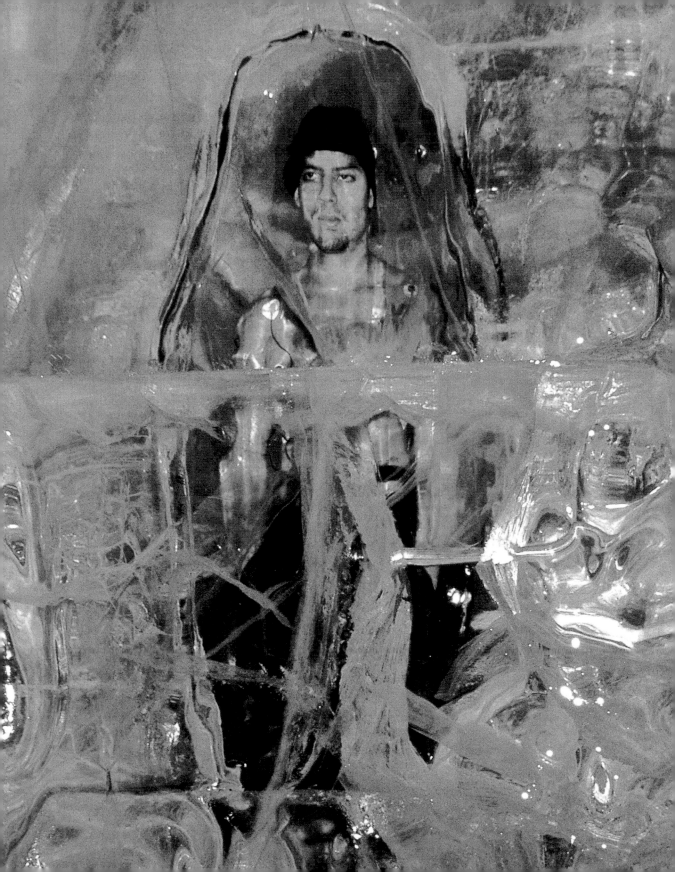

When I do these things I'm not really thinking that I have a chance of dying. For me, it's more creating a performance piece that is elegant and scary and presents a real challenge to be overcome. In a way it's my attempt to reach for an absolute morality. I feel the most honest and pure when I do challenges, because at those times I'm living minimally—freed of all the things that we're fooled into believing we need.

Besides, these endurance stunts aren't meant to challenge only myself—they depend on the active involvement of the audience. My performances are all about confronting our collective primal fears and, in the process, reinforcing our common humanity. When someone does something truly extraordinary, we can all feel a little bit better about ourselves, a little prouder of being members of the human race.

I started training for the ice in Las Vegas. Tom Bramlett, who had worked with me on Buried Alive, had a hollow rectangle of ice built outside a warehouse on the outskirts of the city. Wearing only shorts, I climbed up a ladder and lowered myself into the ice. Within an hour a crowd had formed around my giant ice cube, staring at me. First it was just kids, but they ran home and got their mothers. Then all the people from the neighboring businesses stopped work and came over to stare. After a few hours there must have been sixty to seventy people milling around, compelled and fascinated by the image of a man embedded in a block of ice.

Right then I knew that my instincts about doing this stunt were right, but it was hard to communicate that to Bramlett because, after seven hours in the practice cube, my body temperature had dropped, I was incredibly drowsy, and I was slurring my words. Even after soaking in a hot tub for two hours, I was still shivering. In fact, I wound up shivering on and off for the next fourteen hours, but that just made me want to do this even more. Bramlett, concerned about the dangers, told me he thought it was possible to get ice thick enough so I could stay inside it for twelve hours. I told him to make it twenty-four hours, and he agreed. It was months before he read

the papers and found out that I was going to stay in the ice for three days.

While Bramlett and his crew went to work obtaining the ice and designing a way to support it, I went back to New York to train. We prepared for more than six months. At first, it was just doing things that would help me acclimate to the cold. I rode my motorcycle in the dead of winter wearing only a T-shirt. At my gym they set up a huge tank filled with ice and water, and I began to take daily baths, gradually increasing the time I spent in the freezing mixture. I'd even take ice baths at home, too, something I remember reading that Houdini would do before his bridge jumps.

Besides preparing for hypothermia, there was another concern with the ice stunt. Simply staying awake for three days straight could seriously impair my mental acumen and judgment. Every person needs a different amount of sleep per night to function. Albert Einstein, aware of his sleep needs, slept ten hours a night to ensure optimal performance. Winston Churchill had to have a full night's sleep, and he supplemented that with daily naps. Thomas Alva Edison, on the other hand, was convinced that sleeping was a throwback to our "cave days." He catnapped in his laboratory while holding a heavy ball bearing. As soon as he fell into a deep sleep, his grip would loosen, the ball bearing would hit the floor with a re-

This drawing was for a proposed water stunt in Times Square. When I saw it, I realized it should be an ice challenge.

sounding thud, Edison would be jarred awake, and he'd resume working.

I'm no Edison. I normally sleep seven hours a night. Recent studies have shown that if you miss as little as a few hours of your normal sleep time per night your body's ability to process carbohydrates, manage stress, and fight off infections is significantly impaired. The effects of pronounced sleep deprivation are pretty bad. In 1959 a New York disc jockey named Peter Tripp spent 201 sleepless hours (almost eight and a half days) broadcasting from a booth in Times Square as part of a charity fund-raising event. When he began to fall asleep, nurses shook him. After just a few days of sleep deprivation, he started to hallucinate. He saw cobwebs on the broadcasting equipment. Imaginary mice and kittens nipped at his feet. He even insisted that a technician had dropped a hot electrode into his shoe. He broke the then-existing record for sleep deprivation, but it came at a heavy cost. He lost his job, his marriage ended in divorce, and he bounced around the radio industry for the rest of his career, taking a succession of journeyman jobs. It seems that his judgment was permanently impaired by his endurance stunt.

(above) *Diane Sawyer and Charles Gibson of* Good Morning America *interview me just prior to my entombment in the ice.*

To guard against sleep deprivation, I began to learn how to sleep standing up. Every night when it was time to go to sleep, I'd lean against the wall in my bedroom, touching it with only the top of my forehead. I'd fall asleep and have surreal dreams of falling off cliffs. But I *was* falling, and right before I hit the floor I'd wake up. After a few weeks of slamming into the floor in the middle of the night, I finally learned how to sleep lightly and

make it through the night without toppling over.

Now the problem became finding a location for the ice. My next television special was to be pre-produced and aired around the stunt. There would be filmed magic segments interspersed with live segments of the ice challenge, culminating in my live extraction at the end of the one-hour special. It turned out that ABC owned a building at Broadway and Forty-fourth Street, in the heart of Times Square, with a street-level studio designed so that the outer walls could be removed, opening right onto the street. It was open at all times to the public, and anyone could come by to witness it with their own eyes. After we had the location, I found out that, by a strange coincidence, the premiere of Houdini's film *The Man from Beyond,* in which he played a man who had been embedded in ice, had been at the Times Square Theatre, just two blocks south.

In October 2000, a month before the event, we started to do practice runs in Nyack, New York. After a while I worked up to staying in the ice for twelve hours at a time. One day my best friend and his girl came to see me and were shocked when they were ushered into an ice locker. The sight of me encased in this block of ice, looking like a zombie, made my friend really upset. Most of my friends were dead set against me going through with this. They told me that I didn't need to torture myself, but they didn't understand. Eventually they realized that there was nothing they could do to stop me and they became supportive.

Vaseline was used to trap my body heat.

In addition to the concerns of my friends, no doctor we consulted wanted any part of this event. The threat of hypothermia was obvious, but they were also worried that blood clots could result from standing in a confined space for three days. There are many documented cases of airline passengers who sit still during long flights and develop blood clots in their feet that then migrate to their brains and kill them. The doctors insisted that, if I went ahead with the challenge, I should try to minimize the danger of clots by having special boots manufactured that would simulate walking, thereby pumping the blood up from the soles of my feet. We finally realized that if I did stretching and flexing exercises with my feet, the same effect could be accomplished.

But the doctors were still wary about both muscle spasms and frostbite of the toes and fingers. If I fell asleep leaning against the ice, the risk of frostbite could increase substantially. I didn't want to say anything to the doctors, but I was already anticipating that I might have some form of damage, like losing a toe to frostbite.

Finally, the doctor who'd consulted with us on the Buried Alive stunt signed on. He participated only on the condition that I allow sophisticated sensors to be attached to my body so my vital signs could be constantly monitored. He also insisted that I swallow a high-tech pill previously given to astronauts that could detect and transmit my core body temperature. Even still, the night before the event, my doctor handed me a release form that absolved him of any responsibility if I was to die. He said it was his wife's idea. She happened to be a lawyer.

The training at Nyack went well. When I hit sixteen hours at a stretch in the ice, I stopped. Why suffer through another forty-six hours when I'd only have to replicate the feat a month later? I wasn't going to quit once I was placed inside that ice—end of story. The only real debate we had in Nyack was over the ice itself. Tom Bramlett liked the surrealistic look of the manufactured ice we had been using, but I didn't think it was clear enough. We finally decided to use real glacier ice harvested in Alaska. An ice company filled a semi truck with about thirty thousand pounds of ice and shipped it down. The ice was amazing. It was so crystal clear that a four-foot chunk looked at most four inches thick.

I always put off everything till the last minute, so the day before the event I went shopping for a nice warm ski cap and a good pair of boots. I had already fasted for four days, but the night before my en-

IF THY 'F

tombment I drank a laxative so my system would be completely flushed out. It was a real mistake. I spent the next eight hours in and out of the bathroom, so I didn't get any sleep at all that night.

It was unseasonably warm for November 27. Bramlett and his crew of ice sculptors had already been on-site for a day, setting up the ice. The core temperature of the natural ice from Alaska was about 5 degrees above zero, so the ice had to temper before it could even be cut. This magnificent ice also had to be protected from direct light since any excess ultraviolet rays would swiftly crack and fog it.

There were press people lined up in Times Square that morning, so I answered their questions and let them examine the ice block and the area before I went in. Then I climbed into position to be sealed into the ice. I was wearing only thin ski pants, the boots, and the cap. I had planned on wearing kneepads under my ski pants so I could lean into the ice and relax from time to time, but I was so rushed getting ready that I forgot to put the pads on. At the last minute Bramlett was uneasy that I was going into the ice bare-chested, so I let him tie a long-sleeved shirt around my waist.

Finally it was time. I positioned myself in the center of the ice. My crew had previously taken a mold of my body and precut the ice into two pieces. They slowly moved the six-thousand-pound pieces

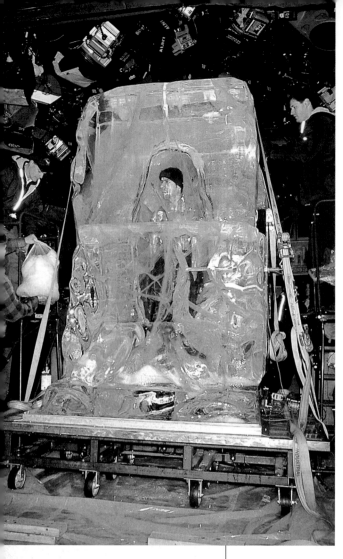

A TV program accused me of slipping out of the ice into a chamber below. This was obviously not possible.

of ice toward me. It seemed like an eternity, but finally the two pieces enveloped me. I'll never forget that eerie sound, that slow, drawn-out *crickk*, as the two massive ice blocks melded together, sealing me into my frozen vertical coffin.

I was immediately claustrophobic. There was something wrong; the ice was only half an inch away from my nose. In the practice runs I'd always had more room than that inside the ice, but because of concerns about the high temperature that day, less ice had been carved away. I was also incredibly cold because Dr. Ruden had given me blood thinners that lowered my body temperature. My whole body started shivering; my adrenaline started pumping, and my heart felt like it would beat right through my chest. There was no way I would ever be able to get through this, I thought.

Then I calmed down. I accepted where I was and what I was doing. I saw my brother and Kalush and Josie through the ice (they stayed on-site for the entire time), and even though I couldn't stop shivering, I knew I had to get through this. I figured that the air would eventually feel warmer since some air was being pumped into my frigid chamber from the outside. When we did the trials in the ice locker in Nyack, the air that was pumped in was about 26 degrees. It was unbearable, but because it was so unseasonably warm out, the ambient outside air would probably be a little more comfortable.

I had some other comforts, too. Because dehydration was a big concern of the medics, we had rigged a tube that would feed me hot tea, but the first time I sucked on that straw, the tea was scalding, and I wound up burning the roof of my mouth. At least that temporarily distracted me from the numbing cold. The first few hours were unbearable. I didn't even notice the crowds that were steadily filing past me. Being entombed in ice was a completely different experience from being buried alive. There was something comforting and secure about lying down in a controlled temperature in a coffin, but standing up in a cube of solid ice was just sheer torture. I was too wired to try to sleep, even though we had put some padding into my ski cap so I could lean my head against the ice without getting frostbite.

I coped with the whole experience by fantasizing. Some people might fantasize about lying out on the beach in Malibu, soaking up the sun, but I went the opposite route. Every one of my fantasies over the next three days involved me as some kind of prisoner of war or victim of a dreadful disease. That was my reality in the ice.

Although time seemed to be going by pretty slowly, by the end of the first day I was able to relax a little and even enjoy the people parading past. A few women walked up to the ice, lifted their shirts, and flashed me, but by the second day in the ice, things began to go pretty bad. The unseasonably warm temperature was melting the ice and, as a result, I found myself a victim of the worst form of Chinese water torture—melted ice slowly and steadily dripping onto my exposed neck and back. After a day and a half of that, I was ready to crack. Then I remembered the shirt that Bramlett had tied around my waist. Somehow I maneuvered it on, and it probably saved my life. I know that I never would have survived two solid days of that torment.

What I didn't know was there was a battle raging behind the scenes. Because the ice was melting so rapidly, there was a real chance that the whole structure could implode, and suffocate me in the process. As far as Bramlett was concerned, I had been in the ice for twenty-four hours—anything more might endanger my life, especially under these circumstances, but Kalush and the other producers heeded my wishes and convinced the ice sculptors to make a mixture of dry ice and snow and delicately rebuild the top of the ice so that it could maintain its structural integrity and not cave in on me.

Then everything quickly went downhill. Because there was no drain in the studio, one of the production assistants was assigned the job of vacuuming the water off the floor. He was in the middle of doing that when I felt a sharp tug and an unbearable burning sensation in my groin. I screamed so loud that Kalush later told me he heard it in an interior office where he was in the middle of a meeting. It turned out that while the production assistant was vacuuming the water off the floor, he accidentally also vacuumed the tube that carried my urine out of the ice. Unfortunately for me, that tube had been glued onto my privates. This was one nightmare scenario I didn't even have to invent.

The New York Times.

A TV Feat by a Reeaally Cool Guy

By JESSE McKINLEY

Shirtless and encased in a block he dares not touch.

High Temperatures Shrink Ice Man's Cocoon

By JESSE McKINLEY

DAY ONE

DAY TWO

As David Blaine spent a second day inside his block of ice, a crowd swelled outside the ABC studios on West 44th Street on Times Square. Organizers said they believed more than 25,000 had come by to see the stunt.

Quick! More dry ice! A stunt is melting!

By the third day I was a total wreck. Lines from some of my favorite movies started playing in my head like an endless tape loop. I kept hearing the dialogue from the famous Russian roulette scene in *The Deer Hunter.* I wasn't even sure if I was thinking it or actually reciting it. The last eight hours were the most horrifying part of the experience. I'd see someone on the line pass by me, and I'd beg him to tell me the time. He'd say, "Two o'clock." I'd wait as long as I could, which felt like hours, then I'd ask someone else the time. "Five minutes after two," she'd answer. I was convinced they were messing with my mind. Something was.

I couldn't control my thoughts. I started seeing things. I hadn't slept a minute for over four days now, and my mind began going to a place that I never believed existed (a place so scary that today I can totally empathize with anyone who suffers from mental illness). One minute I knew where I was, the next minute I was convinced that the ice event had happened months ago. Then I started to feel strange and my vision got blurry. Suddenly my mind

TOM BRAMLETT: *I was ready to chop his ass out of there after twenty-four hours. Just because he agreed to do it for three days didn't mean I did. I knew he lost it on the third day when I was propping up the melting ice near the block and I heard a funny sound. It was David singing that "Oooh wee oooh" song from* The Wizard of Oz. *Then he pulled the sensors that were monitoring his blood pressure and heart rate right off. I didn't like that at all.*

BILL KALUSH: *By the end, David stopped responding to our hand signals, so we lost all communication. He just wasn't there mentally. It was about time to get him out of the ice, but instead of using the chain saws, the director had the ice guys use a little scraper, like something you'd use to scrape the ice off your*

188 DAVID BLAINE

Magician Emerges From Icy Stunt

By JESSE McKINLEY

After nearly 62 hours trapped inside an ice cage of his own devising, a wan and weak David Blaine emerged last night in front of a live television audience and several thousand screaming fans in Times Square.

With a driving rain soaking spectators, Mr. Blaine, 27, was cut out of the ice box by a chain saw at 10:50 p.m., ending an ordeal he began early Monday morning on the set of ABC's "Good Morning America" on West 4th Street. The magician who emerged from the increasingly unstable ice box seemed a shadow of the confident, robust, shirtless fellow who entered two days before. Immediately after his exit, Mr. Blaine, wrapped in blankets and a robe, was rushed by ambulance to a doctor's office on the Upper East Side for an examination.

He managed few words despite a horde of cameras and reporters. "Must go to sleep," he said, lying on a stretcher. "Can't talk, can't think."

The escape was the culmination of a stunt that Mr. Blaine said he had undertaken to "challenge every human fear." In this case, Mr. Blaine apparently addressed the fears of those unlucky souls who harbor phobias about becoming trapped in a giant ice box.

Standing nearly motionless in a carved-out air cavity inside the six-ton block of ice, Mr. Blaine flirted with several serious medical dangers, including hypothermia and blood clots. Last night, his medical adviser, Dr. Ronald Ruden, seemed especially worried about frostbite, as Mr. Blaine's feet had soaked in melted water. "I'm concerned about his feet,"

David Blaine looked out from a hole cut in his ice block before he was removed last night at the end of a nearly 62-hour stunt.
Kevin P. Coughlin for The New York Times

DAY THREE

of the chill appeared to have been lost for Mr. Blaine, who looked pale and cold inside his ice bubble, often putting his hands in his pockets or blowing into his stocking cap. And unlike previous days, he wasn't smiling much.

Part of his unhappiness had to be stationed themselves on a pedestrian island in the middle of Times Square. Traffic along West 44th was slowed, and police officers continually told onlookers to keep moving. Mr. Kalush estimated that 1,500 an hour were passing by to see Mr. Blaine and his lumpy cube.

windshield. They were scraping a six-ton block of ice with a fifty-cent ice scraper. David started to look pretty agitated, so that's when Bramlett took control and told them to get the chain saws and cut him out of the ice.

BRAMLETT: *Once we started running the saws, David thought it was time to come out. If he even thought at all. At one point, we were coming in with a chain saw and he was so out of it he was trying to grab the blade.*

KALUSH: *We were concerned that the ice was so fragile that if they cut into it too rapidly the whole structure might collapse in on David. So they cut a two-inch-by-two-inch hole and started talking to him.*

BRAMLETT: *We finally got a small hole in it. David wasn't making much sense, but he did say, "Let me out now!" so we started going for it. Then one of the director's assistants came up and grabbed me and said, "Stop! You can't get him out now." I just turned to him and said, "You're not running this anymore. He's coming out right now."*

KALUSH: *One of the people involved was running around saying that if David doesn't walk out and make a speech to everybody, his career is over, he'll never work in television again. Meanwhile, the ice guys had enlarged the hole, and two of them tried to pull David out, but the hole was still too small. They finally enlarged the hole and literally yanked David out. When I saw him come out, I was terrified. I had known David for ten years, but he was like another person. I could tell something was seriously wrong. I was expecting him to complain that he was in pain or something, but he just wasn't there at all. He stared at me, but he was looking right through me. He had absolutely no idea what was going on. That's what scared me. Bramlett actually had tears in his eyes, and that guy's like a big bear.*

BRAMLETT: *I was worried that David would die. He really looked like he was in shock. His skin was burning up, and he was soaking wet. Then they brought him over to be interviewed live.*

KALUSH: *David's incoherent. They're asking him questions live on camera, and he's saying, "Josie. Josie. My mind. Can't talk. Can't think." We threw a blanket over him and rushed him to the ambulance. Remember, we're on live national television and he had come out a few minutes before schedule and I can hear the director screaming in my headphone, "Keep the ambulance door open for more time. Keep him there." I was convinced that David was going into shock*

BREAKING THE ICE: A wobbly David Blaine is assisted last night from the ice block in which he stood for 61 hours. Yechiam Gal

He Blaine, he thaw — he conquered

After 61 hours of hype-o-thermia, David Blaine ended his ice capade on live TV last night.

The magician was helped out of the block of ice in which he'd

an undisclosed location.

A witness said Blaine mumbled the name of his model girlfriend, Josie Marran, as he was put on a stretcher. The stunt was the cli

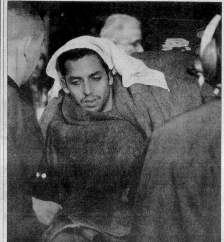

Coming in from the cold
Magician battled his own illusions while in ice

By RALPH R. ORTEGA
DAILY NEWS STAFF WRITER

In the end, it was David Blaine who was mystified after standing nearly 62 hours inside a 6-ton hunk of ice.

"I thought that I had died; I thought that I had woke up and that this was where I was. This was death," the self-proclaimed "mystifier" said yesterday.

Nearly 10 hours after he was freed from his ice block on live television, the 26-year-old illusionist sounded sluggish and sickly as he sat with his feet propped up in his Manhattan apartment.

"My legs, I can't bend or anything. But I think the worst was the sleep deprivation," Blaine told ABC's "Good Morning America."

Blaine was fatigued and dehydrated after his ordeal but in "general good health and spirits," a spokesman said.

Calling the stunt his way of facing "every human fear," Blaine said his 2½ days standing encased in ice was almost too much for him. The narrow cocoon hollowed in the ice was smaller than expected and "unbearable," he said.

"Three hours into it, I said, 'There's no way I'm going to be able to make it,'" he said. "Then I just accepted that I had to do it. And that's when it was like a bad trip started."

There were worries that Blaine — who slept in spurts, drank liquids through a tube and used a catheter — would be susceptible to hypothermia, frostbite or blood clots. But it was hallucinations that tormented him.

At one point, he desperately screamed at his girlfriend, model Josie Maran, who he thought was atop the ice. She actually was standing next to it.

During his last icy hour, Blaine — who spent a week buried underground last year — thought he was inside a coffin.

"Cut now because I think I'm dead!" Blaine shouted to a technician with a chain saw.

Was the stunt, the most demanding of Blaine's endurance tests, worth the reported million-dollar payoff?

The act did little for Blaine's reputation as a magician, but the thousands who came to watch seemed to like it just fine.

"And in the end, that's what really counts," said David Kaplan, 41, an amateur magician from Boston.

"Three hours into it, I said, 'There's no way I'm going to be able to make it.'"

DAVID BLAINE

CHILLIN' Illusionist David Blaine emerged from a 6-ton block of ice Wednesday night in Times Square disoriented and weak. "I thought I had died," he said after his three-day ordeal inside piece of glacier. "This was death."

REUTERS

VIEW TO A CHILL Worker carefully cuts through portion of 8-foot-high glacier chunk that encases illusionist David Blaine last night in Times Square.

ONE COOL CUSTOMER
61-hour ice-capade ends

By JOE WILLIAMS and LEO STANDORA
DAILY NEWS STAFF WRITERS

The iceman cameth from his frozen prison in Times Square and thaw-gone-it — he's a real survivor.

As thousands of gawkers provided a warm reception of applause and cheers, oddball illusionist David Blaine last night was chipped out of a 6-foot-high, 6-foot-thick chunk of Alaskan glacier that had encapsulated him since Monday.

The 26-year-old entertainer, who looked disoriented and in pain, needed paramedics to keep him on his feet, but he still mustered the strength to plant a peck on the lips of his girlfriend, Josie Maran, who was at his side when he emerged.

"Ow! Ow!" Blaine winced as handlers moved him to a stretcher and took off his shoes.

Stunt organizers said they feared Blaine injured his feet by standing for more than 61 hours straight, and that he may have suffered dehydration.

Cold, wet and dog-tired because he was unable to sleep, it was clear Blaine was anxious to end his ice-capade. When workmen appeared to be taking their time chipping him free, he told them, "I want out. I want out now!"

After being locked over quickly, Blaine was deposited in an ambulance and whisked away for a full physical evaluation.

Thousands of spectators ignored a cold and steady rain to gather at Broadway and 44th St. for the event, which was broadcast live on ABC-TV as the finale to

ORDEAL'S OVER Illusionist David Blaine gets help from paramedics last night as he is whisked to a hospital.

---

and that he might die. I really thought that I had just killed my best friend. I pulled everyone away from the ambulance and slammed the door, and the ambulance took off.

My first memory was in the ambulance. I was convinced that the stunt was a huge failure and my career was over. I felt that I had let everybody down by not coming out of the ice strong. The whole time in the ice, I'd been planning to make a little speech dedicating the event to my mom, but when I got out I couldn't even manage that. Dr. Ruden just kept smiling at me, which was tripping me out even worse. He was leaning over me in the ambulance saying, "You have no idea how big this is. You're huge. You're huge." I was getting more and more paranoid by the second.

They rushed me to a doctor's office, where I underwent a comprehensive checkup. No blood clots, no evidence of shock, no frostbite, no hypothermia, no pneumonia. My toes were all intact, although they were numb for the next couple of months and my ankles had swollen to the size of cantaloupes. By the end of the exam, my mind had cleared up, but I was so fatigued they brought me home in the stretcher. A few of my friends were waiting in my apartment to cheer me up, but I was still despondent and paranoid. Where was Kalush? Bramlett? Why wasn't my brother there? It

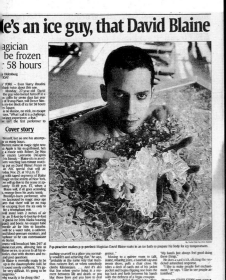

He's an ice guy, that David Blaine

Magician ... be frozen ... 58 hours

Cover story

P-p-practice makes p-p-perfect: Magician David Blaine soaks in an ice bath to prepare his body for icy temperatures.

turned out they all just wanted me to get some rest, but to my paranoid mind they were all too embarrassed by my failure to come over.

I didn't sleep a wink that night. In fact, I didn't sleep for another two and a half nights; then I slept for two days straight. Josie's mom is a nurse, so she was kind enough to help me regain my strength. After a few days homebound, I was still in too much pain to walk, so Josie wheeled me around in a wheelchair. It took a week and a half until I could walk unassisted. A few days after that, I limped onto a plane, and Josie and

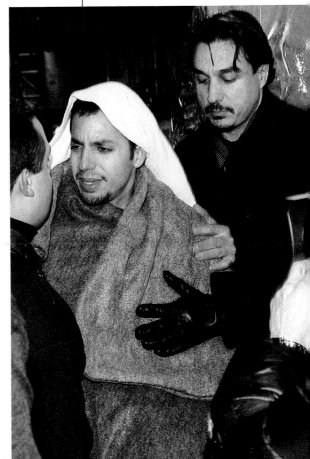

Agony

I went on a vacation. We made sure we went someplace warm.

I was gratified by the amazing reaction to my ice challenge. By the end of the stunt, almost a million people had filed by me. The media interest was intense; even *The New York Times* covered it every day. The website that was set up to transmit a live feed of the ice got so many hits that it had to shut down. Even still, that was the last time I'll ever do an ice stunt. I just can't see putting myself through that kind of torture again.

I can't say I have any regrets about going through with the ice challenge. It's always fulfilling to set a goal for yourself and then achieve it. I wound up shattering the old record of staying in ice, but my stunt never made it into *The Guinness Book of World Records*. They acknowledged that I had broken the record, and they sent me forms to fill out so I'd be included in the next edition, but I still haven't gotten around to completing them. It's funny, I was able to stand in a tomb of ice for 61 hours, 40 minutes, and 15 seconds, but I can't seem to deal with a few minutes of paperwork.

CHAPTER XII

VERTIGO

*When a man sits with a
pretty girl for an hour, it
seems like a minute. But let
him sit on a hot stove for a
minute—and it's longer than
an hour. That's relativity.*

—Albert Einstein

Vertigo

he dictionary defines vertigo as "the sensation of dizziness or swimming of the head," "a difficulty in maintaining an erect posture," and "a reeling sensation; feeling about to fall." Lucky for me, I didn't suffer from any of those afflictions when I was standing nearly ninety feet above Manhattan on a twenty-two-inch pillar for almost thirty-five hours. In fact, for the first time in my life, I had a clear understanding of the world. I realized that this world is just a series of sunrises and sunsets. And that's it.

San Simeon, a fifth-century ascetic monk who also spent a lot of time in the air, had a different conception of the world. He was convinced that the world was so corrupted by evil that he could only escape his decadent times by living on top of a pillar. San Simeon, and the later pillar saints whom he inspired, were called the Stylites, and they were sure that they could overpower the downward tendencies of man's nature by going up. Living high on their platforms, they thought they were closer to God. They also believed that the more the body suffers, the more the spirit flowers.

San Simeon was by far the most renowned pillar saint. He was born around 389 A.D., the son of a Syrian shepherd. He, too, was destined to be a shepherd when, at age thirteen, he became obsessed with interpreting Christ's message. For him it meant suffering persecution, mortification, fasting, humiliation, and tears.

Convinced he should become a monk, he went to a local monastery and begged to be admitted as a servant. To show his dedication, he lay at the gate for five days without food. He was welcomed into the monastery, but he left after two years and moved to a stricter monastery near Antioch. Without the other monks' knowledge, he wore a rope made of twisted palm leaves under his garments that was tied so tight it ate into his flesh. He nearly died of his self-inflicted punishment, and it took three days of soaking before the rope could be cut out of his skin. Convinced he was a zealot, the authorities threw San Simeon out of the monastery.

He then descended into a deep well nearby and refused to eat or sleep. He was close to death when the monks from his last monastery rescued him. Impressed by his dedication, they began revering him as a saint. This made San Simeon uncomfortable, so he left them and moved to a cell made of dry stones and earth at the foot of Mt. Teleanissae near Antioch. Here he began what would be a lifelong practice—he fasted for the entire forty days of Lent. After three years in his cell, he moved to the top of the mountain and lived in a small structure that had no roof. Concerned that mobility would detract from his practices of devotion, he chained himself to a rock. A bishop who feared San Simeon would set a precedent visited him and told him to relinquish his chains, reasoning with him that San Simeon's will alone, with the help of Divine Grace, could serve as restraint enough. By then, San Simeon was besieged by pilgrims seeking his blessings and vying to tear pieces of his tunic to keep as holy relics. His extreme dedication and popularity alarmed the established church authorities, and he was threatened with excommunication.

In 423 A.D., when he was thirty-three, he began to live on a six-foot-square platform on top of a nine-foot pillar that his disciples had labored to build for two years. He stayed there for four years, then moved to an eighteen-foot pillar, where he resided for three years. He spent the next ten years on a thirty-three-foot pillar. Finally, his followers built him a magnificent sixty-foot pillar complete with a railing around the platform. He lived there for twenty years.

Scholars maintain that San Simeon's intent was to escape the world by going up. I myself don't believe that. In reality, rather than distancing him from humanity, the image of San Simeon standing on his pillar was so strong and so unique that the world beat a path to his pole. Beggars came for his blessings, the lame came to be healed, litigants came to get advice on resolving their disputes, even princes came for his counsel on matters of state. He was said to have reconciled enemies, manifested gifts of prophecy, and cast out devils. But more often than not, he stood and prayed. He cut a solitary figure before dawn, his arms and his eyes raised to heaven in prayer. At other times, to display his devotion, he prostrated himself while he prayed, bowing so low that his forehead nearly touched his feet.

He spent thirty-seven years on his various pillars. On September 2, 459, San Simeon was found dead, clinging to the railing of his platform. But his example inspired hundreds of others to replicate his feats, and for five centuries, other monks climbed on top of pillars to live out their lives. One, St. Alypius, remained on his pillar for sixty-seven years without a break. Some of San Simeon's followers built pillars and lived inside them. Other hermit monks moved to mountaintops and sat in one spot for years, never deviating in the direction they faced. Each made their own unique sacrifice, demonstrating, in the words of one tenth-century Stylite: "the hermit's eternal gift of love: denial brings us God."

It's ironic that the Stylites became a significant part of humanity by trying to escape it. In a way, that had also been the case with every stunt I had ever done. This one—"Vertigo"—would be no exception. I was going to stand on a twenty-two-inch-wide pillar in Bryant Park, a beautiful New York City park that borders Forty-second Street, one of the most famous streets in the world. The pillar was about eighty-three feet off the ground, so I was looking down from a height of close to ninety feet. I would stand on this pillar for thirty-five hours with no food and virtually no liquid. For thirty-three of those hours, there would be nothing beneath me except steel and concrete. If at any point during that time I fell, I would die. There would be two handles coming out of the pillar that were on a hydraulic lift, so that they could be raised when I needed to do stretches, which would be about once every four to six hours. During the last two hours of this challenge, my support team would build a big catcher out of ordinary cardboard boxes. When they were in place, I was going to return to Earth by jumping into the boxes.

Like any of my challenges, the idea for Vertigo continued to evolve right up to my last second on the pillar. The concept began forming when I decided that I wanted to do a stunt up in the air. When I was a young child, I saw an enormous bird fly up to the top of a flagpole and just stand there. That image was spectacular, and it has always stuck in my mind. But when I started conceptualizing this stunt, my first idea was to erect a plank extending off the top of a building and have police officials put chains around my body and handcuffs on my wrists and then push me off the plank. I was out in L.A. having lunch with my friend Guy Oseary when I told

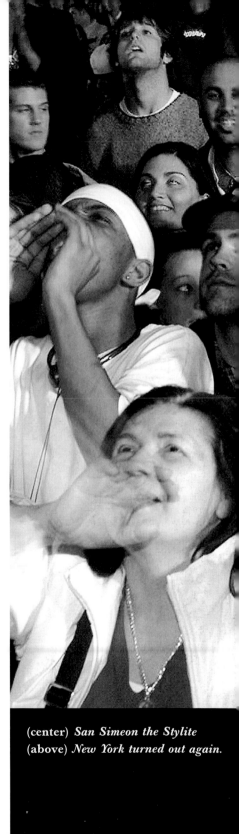

(center) *San Simeon the Stylite*
(above) *New York turned out again.*

9/11/01

him my plans. "David, it's too much. I don't get it," Guy said.

He was right. The most effective magic is magic that can be described in one short sentence. "He floated," or, "He put his hand through a window and took something out." This certainly wasn't that. Looking out the window of the restaurant, Guy pointed to a huge telephone pole. "What about something like that?" he asked. Right at that moment, it came to me. It made sense that I should stand on top of one of those huge scary-looking telephone poles.

When I started doing research on the idea of standing on a pole, I came upon the pillar monks and really liked the idea of connecting this challenge to that rich historical tradition. If it had been up to me, I might have stood on that pillar for as long as some of the Stylites, but I encountered resistance from the people closest to me. My entire team told me they would refuse to work on this challenge if the plan proved to be too dangerous. So we eventually settled on my staying up there for about a day and a half and then jumping off from eighty feet.

I started serious training a year before the stunt and began by standing on the ledges of various roofs. I'd let my feet extend over the edge and then see how long I could stand there before the height affected me. The height never did spook me, but my legs would get tired. The only time I would react adversely was when there was a gust of wind. Eventually, the handles solved that problem. If it got too windy, I could crouch down and hold on to them.

I worked on my endurance and built up my leg and thigh muscles and conditioned my entire body by walking around the streets

of New York wearing a sixty-five-pound chain-mail suit made of stainless-steel links. I knew I could stand in one spot for thirty-five hours, but I was worried about how to combine that with a jump from eighty-some feet in the air. To survive a jump of that magnitude, I had to learn how to free-fall, so I enlisted the help of Bob Brown, the four-time World Cup–champion professional high diver. Bob had spent the last twenty years doing movie stunts, including his famous motorcycle ride through a window onto a helicopter in *Terminator 2*.

I was supposed to begin training with Bob on September 11, 2001. I was scheduled to fly from Kennedy Airport on American Airlines at noon, but that morning my phone rang and a friend said, "Look out your window." I looked and saw smoke pouring out of one of the Twin Towers downtown. I thought that there had been a horrible accident, but as I was watching the disaster, I saw a second plane crash into the other tower. Immediately, I realized that we were being attacked and I ran up to my roof, climbed up on the ledge, and looked down on the streets. It was a surreal scene. People were standing around in clusters, immobile, staring up at the huge burning buildings. Then the first building collapsed, and I fell to my knees, crying.

Of course, the airports were shut down that day, and many of the streets were closed to traffic. Two days later, I hooked up with a friend of mine who owned a private jet and who had business to do on the West Coast. We drove down to Washington, D.C., but all the airports there were still closed, so we were sent by the Secret Service to Baltimore, where we got clearance to depart.

Bob Brown's training facility was in Simi Valley, about a forty-five-minute drive from L.A. I spent the next four months working out at least five times a week with Bob and his team. We did trampoline work, mountain biking, kayaking, and weightlifting. But most important, I began to learn how to free fall. We started the high jumps at ten feet. Then we did twenty. When we got to thirty feet, it began to get scary. I worked my way up to jumping sixty-five feet into an airbag.

Finally it was time to practice a jump into cardboard boxes. The pioneer stuntmen used to go from twenty or thirty feet into cardboard boxes, but once airbags came along, the level of high-jumping increased dramatically. Airbags were a lot safer and a lot softer, but there was something about the boxes that attracted me, even though

it worried Bob that boxes don't react the same way every time. If I didn't land perfectly flat on the boxes, it would be a catastrophe. If I landed feet first or balled up, I'd knife right through the boxes and most likely break my back. If I pulled back too early and continued going backward, there was a good chance I would break my neck. I was really worried that I was going to hit wrong and end up paralyzed. Then there was the unthinkable scenario. Bob told me that he had five friends who weren't around anymore because they had messed up at eighty feet (and they hadn't even had to stand in one spot for more than a minute).

I tried not to think about all this when I climbed up onto the small one-foot-square platform forty feet above the boxes that had been assembled on the ground. The wind was whipping through Simi Valley, and I looked out and saw the prize bulls that were grazing nearby. I listened for the count, and I jumped. Seconds later, I was ripping through the stack of boxes. When I stopped, I was within six inches from the ground. If I had been eighty feet high, I would have broken my back, no question. As it was, I fractured a rib and suffered severe whiplash. That was my last jump for over four months.

I stayed in L.A. for a few weeks, wearing a neck brace and consulting with Bob's chiropractors. After I healed, I flew back to New York and started filming the prerecorded magic segments for the Vertigo TV show, but because I was concerned about my need to continue training for the stunt, which I felt would be life-threatening, we didn't have much time to film. I went back to California about a month before the airdate to resume training, but every time I jumped, I hurt my neck, which was still weak from the previous injury. Finally, Bob took me aside and explained to me that when you're in the air, it's hard to get your balance because there's nothing grounding you. He knew that I ride a motorcycle, so he suggested that while in the air, I lean back as if I were doing a wheelie on my bike. That made immediate sense to me, and after that I nailed every practice jump.

After two more weeks I was ready. I flew back to New York about a week before the challenge. I had already begun cleansing my system in anticipation of my ordeal, so I had restricted my diet to organic cucumbers, red peppers, and water. I was scheduled to go up on the pillar at around noon on Tuesday, May 21, so by Saturday I had started a total fast, surviving only on water. Sunday night I took a laxative to clean out my system, so I didn't get much sleep. Then on Monday night, the night before the challenge, I couldn't really sleep much, either.

The morning of Vertigo, I spent some time with my closest friends. Before doing a stunt, I usually become paranoid if I'm thinking something might go wrong or if I have negative thoughts. When that happens, or even when I hear someone say a disquieting phrase, for instance, "brain tumor," I have to find a piece of wood and knock on it for good luck. That morning I was so superstitious that I told Tom Bramlett to find me a small piece of wood that I could bring up with me onto the pillar. It's funny—Bill Kalush was urging me to bring up water, but all I wanted to carry up there was that small piece of wood.

Finally, it was time. I walked across the lawn to where the pillar was set up. My main concern was saying good-bye to my friends who had shown up, but there was a huge throng of press people there, so I answered a few questions. The media kept asking me why I would do something like this, and I knew that it was the question a lot of people were pondering. But when you feel compelled to do this sort of thing, you can't really explain it. The best response I can come up with is that I set up goals for myself and then I go out and achieve them. But the press wanted more.

"What happens if your neck hits at the wrong angle?" one reporter asked.

"Then I'm in trouble," I said.

"How will you manage to stay awake?" another asked.

"If your life was on the line, you'd stay awake, too," I said. "If you don't stay awake, you die."

"Any last thing you want to leave us with?" someone asked.

I thought for a second. "Always be amazed by everything. Appreciate everything. Appreciate your mother. Talk to her. That's the one thing I wish I could go back and do again. Appreciate the things that are in front of you, because you never know when they'll be gone."

It was time to ascend. I was wearing the same boots I had worn for the ice stunt, medical stockings that were meant to reduce the threat of blood clots, a pair of comfortable pants, a long-sleeved shirt, and a hooded linen shirt that my friend had designed for me. Going up was the easy part. Rather than just climb up the pole, I had envisioned holding on to the hook of a crane and riding it straight up. The authorities nixed that, so I improvised and jumped onto a huge red wrecking ball. I was wearing my motorcycle gloves so I could hold the cables that connected to the crane. We started lifting up into the air, but the reality of what I was doing still hadn't sunk in, so I wasn't even concerned when the ball tapped the pillar on the way up. Finally we were parallel to the platform, and I casually stepped off the ball onto what was to be my home for the next day and a half.

Everyone asks me what I was thinking those first few seconds I was up on the pillar. But, other than to notice that I was much higher than the surrounding trees, I didn't have any profound insights or emotions up on that pole. You just know you're up there and you have to survive. If I told you you had to stand on a chair for twenty-four hours, you wouldn't get some big rush when you climbed up on top of it. Maybe after hour four or five you'd start to realize what you were going through. It was the same thing for me on the pillar. It's funny: my team always laughs at the fact that most magicians do illusions that look dangerous but are in reality safe and that *I* tend to do stunts that look fairly safe but are in actuality dangerous—except for this one. This one looked dangerous and it *was* the most dangerous challenge I'd ever undertaken. I had to will myself to remain calm and stand in one spot—without food, without sleep, and without much water—all the while warding off vertigo. Of course, to come down I'd have to jump, and jumping from almost ninety feet in the air into cardboard boxes is definitely a physical challenge. How *much* of a challenge I didn't really know, because I had never before attempted a jump after standing in one spot that long—from any height.

Despite all my mental preparation, I had only been up on the pillar for three hours when the pain began to set in. There were sharp pains shooting up and down my spine, as if someone had plunged a knife into the middle of my back. My legs felt like they were asleep, then they just went numb. The soles of my feet started aching. We had anticipated that my legs weren't going to work if I just stood still, so to gain some blood flow and reduce the swelling in them I had the handles lifted and I did some stretches, lifting my legs as high as I could, to keep the blood flowing. When I was done stretching, the handles were lowered back into the pole.

I was determined to get through this challenge without drinking any water. My team was pretty unhappy with that idea, and right before I went up on the pillar, Bill Kalush forced a small bottle of water into my pocket. Three hours into the stunt, something happened that suddenly put the reality of what I was doing into stark relief. The water bottle fell out of my pocket and hurtled toward the ground. I watched as it hit a stage light with so much force that the light exploded. My heart immediately started to race, and I got dizzy and nervous.

Until then, this whole experience had been something of a fantasy. I had convinced myself that in the worst-case scenario, I could fall off the pillar and let my body go limp in order to survive the fall. There are a few documented cases of drunks who have fallen from heights of over eighty feet and lived because they fell like a rubber band, but I had never thought through what the consequences of a fall like that would be. To me, the crucial thing was that they had lived—I didn't allow myself to realize that, though they might be alive, they would never walk again. But when I saw the impact that small half-liter plastic bottle had on that light, the reality of my situation hit me like a ton of bricks. I buckled down and concentrated on my balance. I decided that I wasn't going to move my feet or lean forward or do anything that would put me at risk of falling. Then I took out my piece of wood and knocked on it.

It was amazing to look down and see the incredible mixture of people gathered below me. People of every race, religion, and ethnicity were sitting on the grass, standing around with cameras, debating one another, cheering, sewing, sketching, eating lunch, flirting. Some of them were staring at me; some were oblivious. Watching the scene below helped me get through the first day, for sure. What *really* helped was the simple fact that there was no choice—if I fell, I would die. So, to occupy my mind, I would blur my vision and estimate how many people were in the park. Then I'd blur my vision and look up at the skyscrapers and, using multiplication, count windows. Then the sun went

down, and the wind picked up, and the temperature plummeted to within a degree of the all-time record low for that day in New York history. The longest night of my life was just beginning.

I never expected the temperature to go down to forty-one degrees near the end of May, but I resolved that the weather was just one more thing that I'd have to endure. I had a hood on my shirt and I was wearing my leather gloves, but I still shivered most of the night. My back was on fire and my feet were numb. But these were minor annoyances compared to the first real crisis we experienced: around two A.M. I started to nod off.

I slapped my own face in a desperate attempt to stay awake. When I told my crew that I was in danger of falling asleep, they carried on a constant barrage of conversation aimed at keeping me awake. It also helped that the crowd who had stayed through the night started doing some supportive chants. That really helped keep me focused.

Ultimately, what I'll remember most about the whole experience was just observing the sun and the moon going through their cycles—the cycles of life. It was the most amazing experience—to have nothing to do, no worries about bills or cleaning the apartment, or any of the mundane, trivial details of life. I had to worry about survival, but other than that I was free to watch the sun go up and go down. I really hope that everyone gets the chance, at least one time in their lives, to witness the same thing. It was absolutely spectacular to watch the sunset and see the way the light glimmered off the surrounding skyscrapers. Around four P.M. that first day I

saw the moon come up. I tracked it as it went across the horizon and the sky began to blacken. The sun finally receded, and the moon climbed to its apex. Then at about four A.M., I saw a little glint of light blue barely there on the horizon. At five A.M. it was a tiny bit brighter, and time seemed to expand.

The night was finally ending. I knew the day would give me a renewed feeling of energy. Finally the sun itself peeked out, and I saw the birds react, and everything seemed to get lighter and happier. Even though the sun was out, I was still in the shadows, so I was freezing. I counted the minutes until the sun would make its way across the concrete-and-steel canyon formed by the buildings that surrounded me. At last, the sun burst through a slit and hit me right in the face. I had never appreciated the sun like that before. Its warmth washed over me, and I felt like I had been blessed by God.

My kid brother

Now I started tracking the sun. I knew that the next time it went all the way around and turned black again, I would be done. I just waited and waited, but I wanted so badly to jump. My legs had pretty much stopped working and it felt like I was standing on two sticks, but I knew I had enough energy left in me to do this one jump. I was pretty confident, but about four hours before we were to go live on the air, my team on the ground started having a major concern. I didn't know this at the time, but they began to consider closing the whole stunt down because I had started hallucinating.

From the sleep deprivation, the dehydration, and the general fatigue of standing in one place for over thirty hours, my mind had begun to play tricks on me. I started seeing people in the trees surrounding me. Then I turned around for the first time, and I thought I saw a lion's head in the contours of the building behind me. I recounted these observations to my crew and, even though they didn't react, they began to make preparations that I had never authorized. A new layer of boxes was added. The handles on the pillar were raised to their maximum height—thirty-six inches—against my wishes. It upset me at the time, but in retrospect I can see that they were only trying to take measures that would help ensure my safety. The reality was, the doctors later told me, that I was so severely dehydrated I didn't really have total control over my mind.

The last few hours stretched out to what seemed like an eternity. Finally it was ten o'clock, and we went on the air live. By now the entire area was jam-packed with over fifty thousand people, filling the park and overflowing in all directions into the surrounding streets. This stunt was everything that I had dreamed it would be, and I was going to live up to the challenge.

It was time. It's hard to explain what it feels like to be ninety feet in the air, staring down at cardboard boxes like the ones you might store your off-season clothing in, knowing they're all that stands between you and certain death. I had to trick my mind into believing I was going to jump onto an airbag, or else I never would have been able to make that jump. I don't care how organized the boxes looked, anyone's innate survival mechanism would stop them from taking that leap. So I fooled myself—I had to. I had no choice. I just listened to the countdown, and then I jumped.

I had trained for so long, and my mental focus was so strong, that even though I was hallucinating at the end of the challenge, I was able to pick up on the numerical cues, the countdown, and execute the leap. I don't recollect jumping, but watching it later I could see that I had done everything I was supposed to do. The first thing I remember after being up on the pillar is lying inside that mound of boxes. I wanted to get up and walk out, but my legs were totally gone. I was exhausted. So I just lay there until my team dug through those boxes and reached me.

Bob Brown and Bill Kalush propped me up and assisted me to the front of the stage, where I thanked the crowd for all their support. Then they helped me into a waiting ambulance. In the ambulance, the doctors immediately ordered a saline IV, since I was so dehydrated. At the hospital, they asked me for a urine sample. My urine was a bright orange color, a sign that I was in ketosis and my body was breaking down whatever fat it could find to survive. Then they took some X rays and CAT scans and made sure my lungs were okay. Other than being severely dehydrated and weak, I was fine, so they discharged me. Walking was too painful (it took me two days to be ambulatory again), so the ambulance attendants were nice enough to support me and help me up to my apartment.

Once again, I returned to my home from a challenge so banged up that I couldn't even walk through the front door on my own. But it was nice to realize just how fortunate I am to be in the business of taking my wildest dreams and fantasies and turning them into realities. And I felt that somewhere there had to be an angel looking over me and ensuring my safety. I just hoped that angel wasn't going anywhere any time soon because, deep down inside, I knew this was only the beginning.

After thirty-five hours on the pole, everything was okay.

My Dream Manifesto

In order to live a fulfilled life, one must resist the temptations surrounding them:

- Never overindulge.
- Have few extravagances.
- Resist addictions.
- Respect all life.
- Remember that a mistake is only a mistake when you fail to learn from it.
- Accumulate knowledge. Listen. Read. Observe.
- Visit the ocean.
- Try to interact with all different types of people from all walks of life.
- Wonder and be amazed.
- Love and respect those close to you.
- Learn to love yourself.
- Pursue your dreams and goals with passion. Our potential to create is limitless.
- Don't create a robot that's superior to human beings or it will wipe out the human race.

Suggested Resources

BOOKS RELATING TO MAGIC AND ALLIED FIELDS

Bondeson, Jan. *Buried Alive: The Terrifying History of Our Most Primal Fear*

Bulgatz, Joseph. *Ponzi Schemes, Invaders from Mars and More Extraordinary Popular Delusions and the Madness of Crowds*

Burlingame, H. J. *History of Magic and Magicians*

———. *Magician's Handbook—Tricks and Secrets of the World's Greatest Magician, Herrmann the Great*

Burns, Stanley. *Other Voices: Ventriloquism from B.C. to T.V.*

Cannell, J.C. *The Secrets of Houdini*

Cantril, Hadley. *The Invasion from Mars: A Study in the Psychology of Panic*

Christopher, Milbourne. *Houdini: The Untold Story*

———. *Magic : A Picture History*

———. *Houdini: A Pictorial Biography, Including More Than 250 Illustrations.*

Christopher, Milbourne, and Maurine Christopher. *The Illustrated History of Magic*

Clarke, Sidney W. *The Annals of Conjuring*

Dawes, Edwin A. *The Great Illusionists*

Dennett, Andrea Stulman. *Weird and Wonderful : The Dime Museum in America*

Dewey, Herb, and Jones, Bascom. *King of the Cold Readers*

Drimmer, Frederick. *Very Special People: The Struggles, Loves, and Triumphs of Human Oddities*

Erdnase, S. W. *The Expert at the Card Table*

Frost, Thomas. *The Lives of the Conjurors*

Geller, Uri. *Uri Geller, My Story*

Gibson, Walter B., ed. *The Original Houdini Scrapbook*

———. *Houdini on Magic*

Greene, Brian. *The Elegant Universe: Superstrings, Hidden Dimensions, and the Quest for the Ultimate Theory*

Gresham, William Lindsay. *Houdini, The Man Who Walked Through Walls*

Harris, Neil. *Humbug: The Art of P. T. Barnum*

Hesse, Hermann. *Demian*

———. *Siddhartha*

Hoffmann, Professor (Angelo Lewis). *Modern Magic: A Practical Treatise on the Art of Conjuring*

Hopkins, Albert A., ed. *Magic: Stage Illusions, Special Effects and Trick Photography*

Houdini, Harry. *A Magician Among the Spirits*

———. *Miracle Mongers and Their Methods: A Complete Exposé*

———. *The Right Way to Do Wrong: An Exposé of Successful Criminals*

———. *The Unmasking of Robert-Houdin*

Houdini, Harry, and Patrick Culliton. *Houdini Unlocked*

Howard, Vernon. *The Mystic Masters Speak! A Treasury of Cosmic Wisdom*

Hugard, Jean. *Houdini's Unmasking*

Jay, Ricky. *Jay's Journal of Anomalies*

———. *Learned Pigs & Fireproof Women: Unique, Eccentric and Amazing Entertainers*

Keel, John A. *Jadoo*

Kellock, Harold. *Houdini: His Life Story*

Kunhardt, Philip B. Jr., Philip B. Kunhard III, and Peter W. Kunhardt. *P. T. Barnum: America's Greatest Showman*

Lorayne, Harry. *The Magic Book: The Complete Beginner's Guide to Anytime, Anywhere, Sleight-of-Hand Magic*

Mackay, Charles. *Extraordinary Popular Delusions and the Madness of Crowds*

Monestier, Martin. *Human Oddities*

Nelms, Henning. *Magic and Showmanship: A Handbook for Conjurers*

Price, David. *Magic: A Pictorial History of Conjurers in the Theater*

Robert-Houdin, Jean-Eugène. *Memoirs of Robert-Houdin*

———. *The Secrets of Conjuring and Magic*

Scot, Reginald. *The Discoverie of Witchcraft*

Sifakis, Carl. *Hoaxes and Scams: A Compendium of Deceptions, Ruses and Swindles*

Silverman, Kenneth. *Houdini!!! The Career of Ehrich Weiss*

Smith, Morton. *Jesus the Magician*

Stowers, Carlton. *The Unsinkable Titanic Thompson*

Vernon, Dai. *Malini and His Magic*

Wallace, Irving. *The Fabulous Showman: The Life and Times of P. T. Barnum*

Weltman, Manny. *Houdini: Escape into Legend*

Harmony Korine (left), *director of* Gummo

BOOKS OF INTEREST

Dostoyevsky, Fyodor. *The Brothers Karamazov*

Einstein, Albert. *The World As I See It*

Frankl, Viktor E. *Man's Search for Meaning*

Kafka, Franz. *The Metamorphosis*

Levi, Primo. *Survival in Auschwitz*

Machiavelli, Niccolò. *The Prince*

Orwell, George. *Animal Farm*

Poe, Edgar Allan. *The Unabridged Edgar Allan Poe*

Rand, Ayn. *The Fountainhead*

Saint-Exupéry, Antoine de. *The Little Prince*

Salinger, J. D. *Nine Stories*

———. *The Catcher in the Rye*

Voltaire, François-Marie Arouet de. *Candide*

RECOMMENDED MOVIES

Harold and Maude

Medium Cool

Days of Heaven

Fitzcarraldo

The Deer Hunter

The Night of the Hunter

What's Eating Gilbert Grape?

Gummo

My Best Fiend

Mean Streets

Four Shorts by Werner Herzog

Credits

Mike Segar/Reuters/Getty Images; page 200: Austin Metze;
page 201: 2002 Cable News Network LP, LLLP, an AOL
Time Warner Company; page 202: *Late Show with David Letter-
man*, © 2002 Worldwide Pants, Incorporated, *New York Post*;
page 203: Dennis Van Tine/London Features; page 205: Lea
Bonnier; page 206: *New York Post*, New York *Daily News*; page
207: Mark Mainz/Getty Images; page 210: Chris
Pizzello/AP/Wide World; Some images © 2002
www.arttoday.com

PICTURE-INSERT SECTIONS

SECTION I
Page 1: Courtesy of the George and Sandy Daily Collection;
page 2, clockwise from upper right: The Granger Collection,
Courtesy of Charles Greene's magicgallery.com; Courtesy of
the George and Sandy Daily Collection; page 3, clockwise
from top: Courtesy of Mike Caveney, Pasadena, California;
Courtesy of Charles Greene's magicgallery.com; Courtesy of
the David Stahl Collection; page 4, clockwise from top: *The
Cheat with the Ace of Clubs*, c. late 1620s, courtesy of the Kimbell
Art Museum, Fort Worth, Texas, photographer Michael Body-
comb, 2002; Church of the Transfiguration, Novgorod, Rus-
sia/The Bridgeman Art Library; Courtesy of Charles Greene's
magicgallery.com; page 5: Salvador Dalí, *Christ of Saint John of
the Cross*, 1951, © 2002 Salvador Dalí, Gala–Salvador Dalí
Foundation/Artists Rights Society (ARS), New York (right);
page 7: David Harry Stewart

SECTION II
Page 2: Erik Pendzich/Rex Features; page 3: Brent Stirton/Li-
aison/Getty Images (bottom); page 4: Larry Schwartzwald/Li-
aison/Getty Images; page 5: Ezio Petersen/UPI; page 7:
Lorenzo Ciniglio/Corbis/Sygma; page 9: Andrea
Renault/Globe; page 10: Peter Morgan/Reuters/Corbis (top);
page 12: Ancient Art and Architecture Collection Ltd./The
Bridgeman Art Library; page 13: Erik Pendzich/Rex Features;
page 14: Mark Mainz/Getty Images; page 15: Mark
Mainz/Getty Images; page 16: David Harry Stewart

How to Participate in
BLAINE'S CHALLENGE

All participants in Blaine's Challenge will be deemed to have accepted, and be bound by, these rules and conditions of participation:

1. Open to legal residents of the U.S. (except residents of the states of CT, MD, ND and VT), Canada (excluding the Province of Quebec), and the United Kingdom. Random House, Inc., and employees and the author, David Blaine (the "Sponsors"), the Challenge creators, Bill Kalush and Cliff Johnson (the "Creators"), and their attorneys, agents, employees, and immediate family and household members (related or not) are not eligible to enter.

2. To participate, simply obtain a copy of David Blaine's book, *Mysterious Stranger* (the "Book"), by purchasing it or borrowing it from your library or a friend. Hidden throughout the Book are puzzles, enigmas, and conundrums ("Clues") that, once understood and solved, will direct you to the location of a Treasure Map (the "Map") concealed somewhere in the forty-eight contiguous United States. The Map will guide its finder to an Amulet (the "Treasure"). The first individual or group of individuals ("Participant(s)") who, using their own intellect and skill, solve the Clues, and then locate and obtain the Map and the Treasure, must then follow the instructions and submit the materials required under Rule 6 below to the Sponsors in order to become verified winner(s) and claim the prize. Submissions through agents and third parties will not be valid.

3. Warning: It is not necessary to damage or destroy any real or personal property to obtain the Map or the Treasure, or to otherwise participate in the Challenge. The Sponsors of the Challenge expressly forbid any such conduct by Participants, and will not accept responsibility for any actual or consequential damage to or destruction of real or personal property by Participants. The Sponsors reserve the right, in their sole discretion, to disqualify any Participant who: (a) tampers with the entry process or the participation in, or operation of, the Challenge; (b) violates these rules; or (c) acts in a disruptive manner with the intent to annoy, abuse, threaten, or harass any other Participant or person.

4. The Book was first available to the public on October 29, 2002. The Challenge will run until both the Map and Treasure are found and a winner or winners are verified, or until December 31, 2004 (the "Closing Date"), whichever occurs sooner.

5. The solution to the Clues has been recorded in a handwritten document and will be kept in a secure location. The solution to the Clues will be revealed in editions of the Book published subsequent to the Closing Date.

6. Participant(s) who find the Map and the Treasure must contact the Sponsors by calling the telephone number that is secreted with the Treasure no later than December 15, 2004. Specific instructions for claiming the prize will be provided to such Participant(s) at that time. In order to establish eli-gibility to claim the prize, such Participant(s) will be required to deliver to Sponsor possession of the Map and the Treasure and (except where prohibited by law) to complete, sign, and return an affidavit of eligibility and liability/publicity release within fifteen (15) days of Sponsors' contacting such Participant(s). During that time period, such Participant(s) will also be required to satisfy the Sponsors that their discovery of the Map and the Treasure resulted from their independent solution of the Clues using intellect and skill (as opposed to purely chance), and without resort to any prohibited conduct, without the use of inside or confidential information. Minors must have any such documentation signed by their parent or legal guardian. Permission to publicize the name and hometown of the verified winner(s) must be given to the Sponsors in writing prior to award of the prize, and winner(s) may also be required to participate in publicity (except where prohibited by law). In the case of individuals who collaborate, in order to be eligible to win the prize these multiple Participants must each individually comply with all of the foregoing requirements and agree in writing to share the Treasure and release the Sponsors from any liability in connection with the Participants' agreement with each other.

7. The Participant(s) whom the Sponsors and the Creators, in their sole discretion, have verified as having solved the Clues and found the Map and Treasure, and who otherwise satisfy all applicable eligibility requirements ac-

cording to these rules, will win a cash prize of one hundred thousand dollars ($100,000.00) U.S. In the event that more than one Participant is verified as a winner, the prize will be shared among the Participants in accordance with the Participants' written agreement.

8. All materials submitted to the Sponsors, including the Map and Amulet, become the property of the Sponsors and cannot be returned. The Sponsors will not accept responsibility for misdirected, lost, damaged, or delayed submissions or transmissions or for submissions that are altered, illegible, not postage pre-paid, or otherwise not made in accordance with these Official Rules.

9. The Sponsors shall have complete discretion over the interpretation of the Official Rules and reserve the right to refuse to award the prize to anyone who is in breach of these Official Rules

or otherwise fails to establish their eligibility to the satisfaction of the Sponsors. The decisions of the Sponsors regarding the winner(s), and all matters relating to the Challenge, are final.

10. In the event the Map and/or the Treasure are not found by the Closing Date, or in the event there is/are no verified winner(s), $100,000.00 U.S. will be donated to a charitable organization selected by the author, David Blaine. In such event, the name of the charitable organization will be identified and available to anyone writing to the Sponsors.

11. No transfers or assignments of prizes are allowed. All expenses, including taxes, on receipt and use of prizes and the participation in the Challenge are the sole responsibility of the winner(s). By participating in the Challenge, each Participant releases Sponsors, the Creators, and each of their respective parents, affiliates, subsidiaries, suppliers, and agents

from any and all liability for any loss, harm, damages, cost, or expense, including without limitation property damages, personal injury and/or death (except where under applicable law liability for death or personal injury cannot be excluded), arising out of participation in the Challenge or the acceptance, use, or misuse of the prize. Participation in the Challenge and all matters relating thereto is governed by New York State law without reference to choice of law rules, and the Courts situated in that State shall have exclusive jurisdiction over all disputes arising from the Challenge.

12. For the name(s) of the winner(s), send a self-addressed, stamped envelope by April 1, 2005, to the attention of: "Blaine's Challenge Winners List" and mail it to the Sponsors, David Blaine and Random House, Inc., at the following address: Villard Books, a division of Random House, Inc., 1745 Broadway, New York, New York 10019.

International Registry; Imbroglio 332.333.343; Interchange 222.332.232.